Dark Psychology

----- ❧☙❧☙ -----

3 Manuscripts How to Analyze People, Manipulation and Hypnosis

David T Abbots

**Copyright 2018 by David T Abbots
- All rights reserved.**

The follow book is reproduced below with the goal of providing information that is as accurate and reliable as possible. Regardless, purchasing this eBook can be seen as consent to the fact that both the publisher and the author of this book are in no way experts on the topics discussed within and that any recommendations or suggestions that are made herein are for entertainment purposes only. Professionals should be consulted as needed prior to undertaking any of the action endorsed herein.

This declaration is deemed fair and valid by both the American Bar Association and the Committee of Publishers Association and is legally binding throughout the United States.

Furthermore, the transmission, duplication or reproduction of any of the following work including specific information will be considered an illegal act irrespective of if it is done electronically or in print. This extends to creating a secondary or tertiary copy of the work or a recorded copy and is only allowed with express written consent from the Publisher. All additional right reserved.

The information in the following pages is broadly considered to be a truthful and accurate account of facts and as such any inattention, use or misuse of the information in question by the reader will render any resulting actions solely under their purview. There are no scenarios in which the publisher or the original author of this work can be in any fashion deemed liable for any hardship or damages that may befall them after undertaking information described herein.

Additionally, the information in the following pages is intended only for informational purposes and should thus be thought of as universal. As befitting its nature, it is presented without assurance regarding its prolonged validity or interim quality. Trademarks that are mentioned are done without written consent and can in no way be considered an endorsement from the trademark holder.

Your Free Gift

As a way of saying thank you for your purchase, I wanted to offer you a free bonus E-book called **5 Incredible Hypnotic Words To Influence Anyone**

Download the free guide here:
https://www.subscribepage.com/b1b5i8

If your trying to persuade or influence other people then words are the most important tool you have to master.

As Humans we interact with words, we shape the way we think through words, we express ourselves through words. Words evoke feelings and have the ability to talk to the lister's subconscious.

In this free guide, you'll discover 5 insanely effective words that you can easily use to start hypnotizing anyone in conversation.

Listen to this book for free

Do you want to be able to listen to this book whenever you want? Maybe whilst driving to work or running errands. It can be difficult nowadays to sit down and listen to a book. So I am really excited to let you know that this book is available in audio format. What's great is you can get this book for FREE as part of a 30-day audible trial. Thereafter if you don't want to stay an Audible member you can cancel, but keep the book.

Benefits of signing up to audible:
- After the trial, you get 1 free audiobook and 2 free audio originals each month
- Can roll over any unused credits
- Choose from over 425,000 + titles
- Listen anywhere with the Audible app and across multiple devices
- Keep your audiobooks forever, even if you cancel your membership

Click below to get started
Audible US - https://tinyurl.com/yyvr5k3e
Audible UK - https://tinyurl.com/yyfzuyzz
Audible FR - https://tinyurl.com/yyagroe9
Audible DE - https://tinyurl.com/yyrgdn5g

Table of Contents

How to Analyze People 1

Introduction 3

Chapter One: What People's Body Language Reveals about Them 11

Chapter Two: Eye Movements and Facial Expressions 27

Chapter Three: Reading People through Their Handwriting 39

Chapter Four: Tips For Unlocking Insights about Other People's Values 49

Chapter Five: Rebranding Yourself Using Body Language 59

Chapter Six: Reading People through Their Words 69

Chapter Seven: Reading People through Their Environment 79

Chapter Eight: Determining Personality through Birth Order 85

Conclusion 95

Manipulation 97

Introduction... 99

Chapter One: Manipulation and Mind Control Techniques 109

Chapter Two: Emotional Manipulation Techniques... 133

Chapter Three: The Body Language of Manipulation 151

Chapter Four: Reading Body Language and Analyzing People 165

Chapter Five: Secret Social and Subconscious Manipulation Strategies ... 183

Conclusion 189

Hypnosis... 191

Introduction... 193

Chapter 1: Hypnosis 101 195

Chapter 2: Hypnosis Techniques 217

Chapter 3: Best Practices....................... 253

Conclusion 267

How to Analyze People

----- ✥❦✥ -----

*21 Fundamental Techniques to Interpret
Body Language, Personality Types,
Human Psychology, and Secretly
Analyze People*

David T Abbots

Table of Contents

Introduction 3

Chapter One: What People's Body Language Reveals about Them 11

Chapter Two: Eye Movements and Facial Expressions 27

Chapter Three: Reading People through Their Handwriting 39

Chapter Four: Tips For Unlocking Insights about Other People's Values 49

Chapter Five: Rebranding Yourself Using Body Language 59

Chapter Six: Reading People through Their Words 69

Chapter Seven: Reading People through Their Environment 79

Chapter Eight: Determining Personality through Birth Order 85

Conclusion 95

Introduction

"You don't need to be a top-notch interrogator to figure out what is going on in someone's head. The signals are always there--all you need to do is know what to look for."- LaRae

You really don't have to be an FBI investigator to read people or know what exactly they are thinking. A person is almost always giving away his personality, attitude, beliefs, ideologies, likes, dislikes, values and more through signals, if you are perceptive enough to catch those signals. I just read an article today about how what you "like" on Facebook can help the social media giant decipher everything from your gender to your sexuality to your relationship status. There are clues everywhere about people, pretty much offered by them consciously or unconsciously.

You don't realize that people are giving away these clues or signals about them because you are not watching out for it. Once you know exactly what to look for while reading people, you'll be more perceptive towards these signals. Trust me; it is as exciting as solving a challenging puzzle. People can be enigmatic and mysterious. However, a smart people watcher can quickly decipher an individual's personality through their verbal and nonverbal clues.

The ability to analyze people drastically impacts the manner in which you deal with them. When you understand how the other person feels and thinks, you can tailor your message in a way that is best understood by the other person.

Did you know research conducted by MIT concluded that body language alone could determine the outcome of negotiations accurately 80 percent of the time? This simply means people are giving away clues about their innermost thoughts and feelings (probably, things in their subconscious which they aren't even aware of) all the time.

Many things account for an individual's behavior, personality, beliefs, values, and attitude, fundamentally childhood experiences, birth order (yes even the order in which we are born impacts our personality), gender roles, genes, peer behavior and more. Indicators of all

Introduction

these factors are evident in the manner in which a person speaks or conducts himself.

While a layman will look at people scratching their nose as a harmless gesture (it can be harmless of course within the context of say a fly sat on his nose), a people analyzer always looks for a deeper meaning within the context. For instance, if a person has been confronted with something and begins scratching his nose, he is more often than not lying. These are simple and seemingly harmless gestures that reveal a lot about an individual.

The key to understanding and profiling people around you is to pause and closely observe them. It is to see beyond what they show, to hear beyond what they speak.

Every person is like an onion. They have different layers of personality that you need to mentally peel to decode their real traits and persona. Some layers are visible to others, while the innermost layers are something known (or at times unknown, even to them) only to them.

There are many things that you need to pay close attention to if you want to read people with the finesse of a professional psycho analyzer. It can be anything from what a particular person does in his or her spare time to his or her hobbies. For instance, if you get to know that a person attends church during his or spare time, you quickly conclude that he or she is religious. If they are regularly contributing to community activities or volunteering during their spare time, they may be philanthropic, empathetic or socially conscious by nature.

Someone who parties may have an endless zest for the good things in life, while someone who spends hours in front of the television may be low on drive. See, even something as seemingly inconsequential as what a person does in his or her free time indicates their personality.

Some psychologists are of the opinion that a person often gravitates towards things he thinks he lacks to compensate for the same. So, you may look for more friends and social approval because you don't believe you are good enough.

Notice how people are keenly interested in zodiac and sun signs? Isn't that an indication of low self-understanding? People are mainly interested in pursuing things to compensate for what they lack or things that take them in the

Introduction

direction of a clear goal. When people don't get attention, they become showy. People who present a tough exterior may do it to hide their painful past of being bullied as children.

There are subtle clues everywhere. You just need to be alert and watch out for them. I'd suggest starting with yourself. Test your knowledge by analyzing your personality. Next, move towards analyzing the personality of people who are close to you. Eventually, move to strangers at supermarket, airports, coffee shops, etc. to sharpen your people insights. It won't happen overnight.

However, with consistent practice, you will be able to quickly tell about a person simply by looking at them or interacting with them for a while. This will help you communicate in a more mutually beneficial manner with the individual. Think about a scenario, where you are going to negotiate a deal. If you identify what the person is thinking or feeling about the deal, you can modify your speech and body language to tackle their reservations or doubts about the deal, thus winning it in your favor in the end.

How to Analyze People

This is what sales professionals, orators, leaders and other influencers do all the time. They understand who they are selling or talking to and then tailor their message to inspire the person's trust.

I know car sales professionals who are trained to look at what's inside your car for clues about your likes. For instance, if they find a golf kit in the back, they'll start a conversation about how they are looking to enjoy a good game of golf this weekend. The passionate golf player is elated that the salesperson is as interested in golf as he or she is- their amazing ice-breaker! What did the salesperson do? He simply observed and got you talking about what you love to build rapport, and eventually get you to buy from him.

Every person has a unique personality that impacts the way we relate to him or her. Does a person exhibit a predominantly introvert or extrovert personality? Is he or she primarily driven by relationships or material goals? How does the person handle uncertainty? What is it that feeds the person's ego? How is the person's behavior when he or she is stressed or frustrated? How does the person behave when he or she is relaxed?

Introduction

Are you ready to read 21 power-packed tips about analyzing a person using a series of fascinating and proven techniques?

Chapter One:
What People's Body Language Reveals about Them

Body language is an inexhaustible source of information about a person's mind. It offers an astounding amount of information about a person's thoughts, feelings, and beliefs. Reading people becomes easier when you know what to look for. We are invariably wired to pick up body language clues even when we aren't consciously aware of it. According to a UCLA research, 7 percent of all communication relies on words, 38 percent comes from our voice, and a staggering 55 percent comes from body language.

Here are some of the most reliable and proven clues for developing greater insights into a person's thoughts and feelings.

How to Analyze People

1. Body Language

Crossed Legs and Arms

Crossed legs and arms are subconscious physical barriers that reveal that the other person is not open to listening to what you are saying or doesn't believe you. Even if they have a friendly smile plastered on their face or speaking in a courteous manner, their gestures tell a different story. Psychologically, crossing arms and feet is a signal of physically and emotionally shutting yourself from what is before you. The fact that it is subconscious and involuntary makes it near accurate.

Genuine Smiles

How do you tell a fake smile from a genuine one? Mouths often lie, but our eyes reveal the truth. A genuine smile often reaches the eyes and crinkles the skin around the eyes to form crow's feet. Many people offer fake smiles to conceal what they are truly feeling. However, look for crinkles near the eyes the next time you want to figure out if the smile is indeed real.

Chapter One: What People's Body Language Reveals about Them

Postures Tell Stories Too

When several people walk into a room, how do you identify the leader or influencer of the group? The effect is mostly determined by the way they walk and their posture. They will more often than not have an erect posture or walk straight, with their shoulders pulled back in an authoritative position. They subconsciously try to occupy as much space as possible or try to fill as much space as possible with their presence to signify power.

Pulling your shoulders behind expands your frame and makes your frame appear bigger. Similarly, slouching is reducing your form and occupies lesser space to reveal powerlessness.

People who shuffle their posture or position often lack self-confidence or direction. This is also true for individuals whose head faces downwards most of the time. If you notice someone with these body language signals, they may need extra motivation and encouragement to boost their confidence. They may be inhibited or unsure of their ideas, and asking them direct questions can help draw these ideas or suggestions out of them.

It's all in the Eyes

Do you recall the time when your parents and teachers scolded you and asked you to look into their eyes while talking? The primary idea was that it is challenging to hold another person's gaze when you are not speaking the truth. They weren't too off the mark. However, now this knowledge has become so widely shared that liars intentionally hold their gaze for longer than required, which should give you a good idea of their integrity. If you are speaking to someone whose unblinking stare is making you uncomfortable, they may be trying to hide something or lying to you.

Excessive Nodding

When you are speaking to someone or group of people, the ones nodding their head in an exaggerated manner are the ones who are most worried about approval. They are deeply concerned about the impression you have of them and, and are eager to gain your approval.

Stress Signals

Clenched jaws, furrowed brows, and stiff necks are often a sign of stress and anxiety.

Chapter One: What People's Body Language Reveals about Them

Irrespective of what the person may be speaking, he or she is under some form of internal discomfort. They may be uncomfortable about the topic of discussion, or they are thinking about a pressing problem that is causing them stress. The idea is to look out for a clear discrepancy between what the person is saying and their body language.

Nervousness and Anxiety

Excessive blinking and facial movements are a sign of nervousness. Similarly, people who are nervous tend to fidget with their hands and don't let them stay in a single place. Tapping fingers and feet are also a sign of nervousness. Notice how people who are nervous almost unconsciously develop jittery feet.

Feet Direction

When people speak or communicate, the direction of their feet is the last thing on their mind, which makes this unconscious act fairly reliable. The direction in which a person's feet point indicates where they are heading during a conversation. So if a person's feet point towards the door even if they are turning and looking in your direction, they want to escape as soon as possible. Notice how when you are engaged in an enjoyable conversation with someone, your foot instinctively steps forward!

Attraction Body Language

I can write an entire book on this one, but it's sufficient to say that there are typical signs that a person is drawn to you. Of course, there are several factors due to which the language of attraction can vary from person to person. However, in general, leaning in the direction of the person you are speaking to or tilting your head reveal that you are interested in the person or conversation.

Another huge subconscious sign that a person is attracted to you is when he or she starts mirroring your actions. Self-grooming gestures such as running their hands through their hair or straitening their tie/scarf or standing too close to you (we'll look at proxemics later) are signs of attraction. However, expression of attraction also largely depends on an individual's personality type. An introvert may express his or her attraction in a manner that is different from an extrovert.

Chapter One: What People's Body Language Reveals about Them

Shaking Hands

A firm handshake or strong grip is more or less a sign of trust and power. The person is looking forward to a positive long-term association. It is a signal that he or she is mentally present and focused on you and will most likely give his or her all to the partnership or association in future. A limp handshake reveals a weak and potentially dishonest persona.

Similarly, when a person shakes his hand with his or palms facing downwards, he or she is trying to reveal their power or authority over you. They are keen to dominate the association and have their way as much as possible.

2. Walk

People who have a heavy gait combined with a low gravity center may signify some sort of pain, frustration or depression. People who are extremely driven and confident, walk fast and in a single direction. Their posture is more upright.

On the other hand, people who walk at a slower pace are more reflective, and there's an internal dialogue going on within them almost all the time. People who are more driven by emotions tend to change their pace or direction often during the course of walking. When people feel vulnerable, they walk with their arms crossed just above the waist.

A person taking more slow and timid steps may be an indication of low confidence or self-esteem. He or she may need more encouragement to be sure of himself or herself. It reflects how people approach life.

You can also predict the dynamics of a relationship simply by observing a couple walking together. If one person walks ahead of the other, he or she is either dominating the relationship or playing the role of a protector within the relationship. They may also want to lead, grab all the limelight and be the more aggressive partner in the relationship. Although, again this can change according to culture (more on cultural context later).

3. Tone

The tone of an individual's voice can reveal plenty about how he or she is feeling. If the person is not speaking in an even tone or there are plenty of inconsistencies in the tone

Chapter One: What People's Body Language Reveals about Them

throughout his or her speech, they are more likely angry, nervous or excited. It can also be a signal of concealing important information.

Similarly, look out for the volume in which the individual is speaking. When people speak in a volume that is softer than their regular voice, something may not be right.

The tone with which a person speaks can give a lot of meaning to the communication irrespective of what he or she is saying. For instance, notice how people say something seemingly nice on your face but their sarcastic or acidic tone is a total giveaway of what they really think about you. These are people who possess a passive-aggressive personality, who want to hit back albeit in a non-obvious, unaggressive manner. The same words can carry entirely different connotations when they are spoken with a different tone and voice inflection.

For example, the manner in which you finish a sentence or the words you emphasize on can mean different things even if you are using the same words. If people finish a sentence on a high note, they are most likely asking a question or inquiring with a sense of uncertainty or suspicious. Similarly, when someone finishes their sentence in a more flat or even note, it means they are making a statement and not raising doubts. This makes the person come across as more authoritative and assured.

Also, take a sentence like, "Did you steal the ring?" It can have different connotations when the person emphasizes on different words. If the emphasis is on the word "you" they are trying to ascertain whether you stole it or someone else did it. On the other hand, if they emphasize on "ring," they are ascertaining whether you stole the ring or something else.

4. Tips for Reading Body Accurately

Establish a Baseline for Analyzing People

It is vital to have a clear frame or baseline for observing a person's behavior. Of course, this is not always possible, especially when you are meeting new people. However, having a baseline for studying someone's behavior offers you greater insights about them. It gives you a more comprehensive and in-depth overview of his or her personality.

Chapter One: What People's Body Language Reveals about Them

For instance, imagine a person you know closely is a hyperactive, fast-thinking individual who is always charged up about doing things. He or she just can't sit still and is always brimming with ideas. Now, a person who doesn't know this bundle of energy will quickly conclude through his body language that he or she is nervous. The fidgety signals, tapping hands, bouncing feet are all typical signs of nervousness. People who haven't established a baseline for the person's basic disposition will be led to believe that he or she is nervous and not hyper-energetic or excited about doing things all the time.

You need to gain more information or understanding of a person's fundamental nature to read their body language more accurately. How do they typically behave or react in different situations and settings? How they speak and express their ideas and emotions? What is the typical tone of their voice when they experience different emotions? Does it transform when they are excited, sad or nervous? How do they communicate their interest and disinterest about a thing? These are all important insights that will help you read the person more effectively. It will reduce potential inaccuracies in analyzing the person.

When there is a clear mismatch in their baseline behavior, you can tell something is not right. You can keep a close eye on nonverbal expression patterns that are not consistent with their normal behavior.

Look For Clue Clusters

The biggest fallacy people tend to make when it comes to studying people through their body language is that they look for isolated clues rather than analyzing a series of clues together. For example, if you read that maintaining eye contact is a signal of confidence and honesty, you'll conclude only on the basis on a person's consistent eye contact that he or she is a confident and truthful individual.

All other signs that point to the opposite direction such as sweating, twitching toes and touching the face frequently (signs of nervousness or dishonesty) will be ignored because you've made a sweeping conclusion based on a single clue. To arrive at a reasonably accurate conclusion about a person's behavior, you have to look out for a group of clues across

Chapter One: What People's Body Language Reveals about Them

posture, gestures, expressions and voice tone. It is easy to fake one clue (for instance maintaining eye contact) to mislead the reader. However, it is near impossible to manipulate a cluster of clues that point to a specific direction.

Context and Setting

Don't jump to a conclusion about people without understanding the context or setting. For instance, a person may be stiff and formal when you meet them at their workplace, and the same person may be extremely gregarious and effervescent when you meet them at an office party at the bar. The setting plays a vital role in reading people. You may conclude that the person who is simply relaxed is casual about his or her work and doesn't take co-workers seriously. It is nothing but the setting that allows him or her to relax and open up.

Similarly, context is also important. A person may sit crossing his or her arms and legs not because he or she is closed to the idea of listening to you but simply because of its freezing cold.

Likewise, a person may be leaning in the opposite direction because they may be uncomfortable with the seating. Sometimes rubbing your nose constantly can simply mean you have a cold. This is why when you depend on nonverbal clues for analyzing a person; identify a minimum of 2-3 signals that point to the conclusion. Also, rely on different nonverbal communication avenues than a single one. Consider a person's voice tone, walk, posture, hand gestures, facial expressions, feet movements, etc. collectively. This will increase your chances of reading a person near accurately.

Consider the setting. For instance, if a person is being interviewed for a job, he or she may simply be nervous, which is why they may not maintain eye contact or run their hand over their face multiple times. This doesn't necessarily mean they are lying.

Cultural Context

Though smiling, maintaining eye contact and other body language expressions are universal, some gestures and expressions can have different connotations and a different culture,

Chapter One: What People's Body Language Reveals about Them

which means we may misread other cultures through our own cultural filters. Have a baseline or cultural context for studying people belonging to other cultures.

For instance, people in the Italian culture are known to be extremely vivacious and loud in their expressions. They gesticulate in an excited and loud manner with a high pitched voice, marked by plenty of shouting. This is their way of communicating affection and enthusiasm.

Someone who comes from a culture where enthusiasm is not openly expressed (think England), may not interpret this non-verbal behavior accurately. Viewing things in a cultural framework or backdrop makes it easier to deal with people across cultures. Similarly, a single gesture can have different interpretations throughout cultures. For example, the thumbs-up sign is a gesture signifying validation or luck in western cultures. However, in some parts of Middle East, it is not considered culturally appropriate to flash the thumbs-up gesture.

Even when it comes to personal space, people from western countries often strive to keep some space or a physical barrier (such as a handbag, etc.) while interacting with strangers or when they meet people for the first time. It signifies that they want their personal space to be respected. Not noting these differences may cost you your international business deals.

Chapter Two: Eye Movements and Facial Expressions

5. Eye Movements

Your eye movements are closely linked with specific areas of the brain to cause certain movements as your brain functions. If I ask to recall the sound of the person you idolized as a child, your eyes will most likely move a little up and then to the left as you visualize your childhood hero.

Then they'll move a little downwards and to the right when you start imagining the voice of your idol. Nope, I am not spying on you. There is a pattern to your eye movements based on which section of the brain is processing information or function at that time. Your brain nerves are connected with the eyes to cause very specific movements when a certain section of the brain is working. Hence, paying close attention to a person's eye movements can reveal a lot about his or her persona.

Visual Memory

When you ask a person about information that isn't easily available in the memory, the eyes will most likely move to the upper left. It means they are trying to recall past information. This is common among people who are more visual learners and depend on their visual memory for pulling out information. When a person moves his or eyes to upper right when confronted with a question, they are more often than not speaking the truth and simply trying to recall information from memory to give you an answer.

When you ask a person where they had been yesterday, and they look to the left instead of right (trying to recall), they are most likely not speaking the truth. Instead of recalling information, they are trying to construct their own version of where they were.

Internal Dialogue

When a person is grabbling with an internal debate or dilemma, they will mostly glance in the direction of the left collarbone. This simply indicates that a person is deeply thinking about something, engaged in an internal conflict or questioning something through an inner

Chapter Two: Eye Movements and Facial Expressions

dialogue. This is the most likely eye movement when you confront a person, and he or she is torn between telling the truth and lying.

Eyes moving laterally from one side to another quickly can be an indication of lying or looking for some form of escape on being caught. It can also happen when people are creating conspiracies in their mind when they think no one is watching or listening.

Recalling Sound

When a person is trying to recall a particular sound, their eyes move in the right lateral direction. This is a neat trick to assess if people are really reciting lines in the mind when they claim to. Notice how small children will have their eyes in the right lateral when they repeat lines/sounds they've heard from their parents or elders.

Similarly, when someone is making up (or lying) about a conversation they supposedly had, their eyes will move in the left lateral direction. It demonstrates the fact that they are creating a sound that doesn't exist in the first place.

Kinesthetic or Feelings

When a person remembers the feeling or sensation or a specific thing, his or her eyes move to the lower right side. You can try this for yourself. Try to imagine the sensation of satin on your body by closing your eyes. You will gradually notice your eyes moving in the lower right direction involuntarily.

Attraction

When a person is attracted to you or is deeply interested in what you are saying, their pupil size will expand. Similarly, when the subject is changed to something that is boring or doesn't hold their attention, the size will contract almost immediately.

Similarly, if a person is blinking more than normal while interacting with you (over 6-10 times a minute), they are most likely attracted to you. The feelings he or she processes in his or her mind towards you subconsciously impacts your blink rate. This is exactly why blinking is closely associated with flirting.

When someone likes you, his or her eyes will shine in your presence. It isn't all romantic;

Chapter Two: Eye Movements and Facial Expressions

there's boring physiology behind it. When we are attracted to someone, our eyes become slightly moist, which in turn allows them to reflect greater light. Thus, on spotting shiny eyes, you should dig deeper and look at other clues indicating attraction.

Looking Upwards and Downwards

Looking upwards and downwards presents seizing up a person or evaluating them either as a threat or a potential sexual mate. It is often offensive to the person who is being seized as comes across as gaining dominance over the person or looking down upon them. It is almost like the person is saying, "you are not as powerful as me, and hence you will surrender to the gaze."

Potential Errors

Again, unlike most people analyzing techniques, this one isn't foolproof. External stimuli such as sound and light can influence eye movements. The pressure to consistently keep eye contact can also lead to inaccuracies in reading people. If you don't discover a clear movement of eyes, watch out for excessive flickering in a single direction.

Also, the way people process information in the minds differs from person to person based on the sense that is most dominant in them. While some people process information visually, others are auditory creatures.

If you ask someone to describe events as they saw it, they may access their visual memory by moving the eyes to the upper left, but if they are fundamentally auditory creatures, they will also form auditory information of the event by moving their eyes in the right lateral direction.

You've got to identify the sense that rules a person before attempting to read their eye movements. How do you do that? Focus on the words they use while expressing their thoughts, feelings, and emotions. Do they frequently use words such as, "I see your point of view, or I see where you are coming from," they are mostly visual creatures? Similarly, when they emphasize on words such as "I hear that" or "I hear you," they are more often than not dominated by the auditory sense.

You also have to determine whether a person is right or left handed because then the two are ruled by different sides of the brain. So if a

Chapter Two: Eye Movements and Facial Expressions

person is ruled by the right side of his brain and is left-handed, the reverse may be true for them. This means, when they recall information, their eyes may move to the right, and when they are making up information, their eyes may move to the left.

6. Facial Expressions

Examine Full Face

Facial expressions comprise multiple regions of the face. For instance, if a person is surprised, typically his or her eyebrows will be pulled up, the upper eyelids will widen, and the mouth will drop open. Again, one of the biggest mistakes people make while reading facial expressions is looking for single expressions in one region of the face without considering the entire face.

For example, raising eyebrows can be a signal of both fear and amazement. If you want to know which of these emotions is causing the person to raise his or her eyebrows, you have to watch out for other facial clues. Sometimes, people also raise their eyebrows while emphasizing certain parts of their speech.

When the expressions associated with one emotion is a subset of emotions associated with another (amazement or surprise is often a subset of the expressions associated with fear), you have to watch out for other clues.

In this example, if a person is scared, their eyebrows will be pulled up (together), with the lower eyelid being more tensed and the corner of their lips will be pulled back. On the other hand, if the person is surprised, their eyebrows will most likely be pulled up, and their jaw will be slightly lowered. Thus looking at the entire face can give you a more comprehensive reading of what the person is feeling.

Micro Expressions

Microexpressions occur in a matter of split seconds, which makes it near impossible to fake. For example, when a person is resorting to deception, his or her mouth will slant a little. Similarly, immediately after they have uttered the lie, their eyes will roll for a fraction of a second. These micro-expressions are so involuntary and subconscious that they cannot be manipulated or contrived unlike say maintaining constant eye contact.

Chapter Two: Eye Movements and Facial Expressions

When a person is lying, the color of his or her cheeks may change slightly and quickly. Similarly, their nostrils may flare and/, or they may bite their lips (a subconscious gesture revealing that they are preventing themselves from blurting out the truth). The eye movements also become quicker. These signals point to the direction that the person is processing false information.

Focus on Fundamental Emotions

A lot of body language newbies make the mistake of associating an increasingly specific interpretation with a facial expression. That's not how expressions work. There may be several thousands of distinct facial expressions, but they don't necessarily convey a specific meaning similar to words. Instead of assigning overtly narrowed down meanings to expressions, watch out for the primary emotion behind these expressions.

For example, if you are asking who ate the chocolates from the fridge last night, don't look for signals like "ABC" expression means he or she hasn't eaten chocolates; while "XYZ" expressions mean he or she has eaten it.

Rather, focus on the seven fundamental emotions, which have been scientifically proven to be linked with facial expressions. The seven basic emotions are fear, surprise, contempt, disgust, happiness, anger, and sadness. If you want to read a person's facial expressions more effectively, concentrate on identifying basic emotions.

Look At Mixed Emotions

We often experience a series of complex emotions and not an isolated emotion. It isn't rare for people to experience a mix of emotions such as anger, frustration, and sadness. Emotional blend facial expressions often combine movements across emotions. This means different facial expressions can reveal different emotions.

Lips

Lip muscles are delicate and keep shifting to reveal a variety of moods, feelings, and reactions. For instance, pursed lips are an indication of stress, frustration, disproval, and tension. They are trying hard to restrain the expression of their emotions by tightening their lips. It is like holding back words by sealing lips. Puckering is

Chapter Two: Eye Movements and Facial Expressions

a sign of desire or seduction. It can also be a sign of uncertainty. Pay keen attention to slightly twitching lips. It can be a signal of cynicism, doubt or disbelief in the situation. A person who is lying can give himself or herself away with a split second twitch of the lips.

Have you noticed how sometimes the corner of a person's lips will rise to a single side of their face (referred to as sneering)? It signifies contempt or looking down upon someone's actions. It's almost as if the person is deriving some wicked pleasure while disapproving your acts.

Nose

While the nose may not be as impactful as the mouth or eyes when it comes to reading a person, its prominent location makes it easy to read. Flared nostrils are an indication of displeasure or rage. An unpleasant thought or visual may also cause a person's nose to slightly wrinkle. It also reveals disproval or looking down upon something.

At times, the nose's blood vessels dilate, thus making it appear redder and bigger, which happens when a person is lying. Your parents weren't too off the mark when they told you about how your nose will grow big when you lie. Scratching nose frequently is also a sign of lying.

Eyebrows

Despite the fact that our eyebrows have few muscles linked to them, eyebrows are one of the most conspicuous and suggestive features demonstrating our emotional state. If the forehead is slightly wrinkled and the person's eyebrows are raised, he or she is surprised or questioning your actions. When the eyebrows are slightly lowered, and the eyes are hidden along with a bowed head, it is an indication of hiding emotions.

Eyebrows that slant inwards while being stretched downwards reveal rage or frustration. It can also be a sign of a deep focus on concentration. If there's a horseshoe-like fold between a person's brows, it can be a signal of sadness or disappointment.

Chapter Three:
Reading People through Their Handwriting

Every individual's handwriting is believed to be as distinct as their persona. People's handwriting can offer in-depth insights of their personality. It's not just what a person writes that reveals a lot about who he or she is but also how they write it. Graphology or the study of analyzing people through their handwriting is a good way to go beyond characters written on paper into the person's mind to understand who they really are! Here are a few tips for reading a person through their handwriting.

7. Size of Letters

This is a fundamental observation that can be made while analyzing a person's handwriting. Large letters are an indication of a personality that is gregarious, outgoing, extrovert and sociable. It can also indicate a false sense of pride, confidence or self-importance. There is a sense of showing something that they are not.

Small letters, on the other hand, can represent a shy, unsure and timid personality. It can also be an indication of intense concentration and meticulousness. Midsized letters imply the person is self—assured, flexible and well adjusted.

Gap between Texts

People who write without leaving many gaps between words and letters indicate his or her fear of being alone. These folks love to have lots of people around them and may even find it challenging to respect other people's personal space. People who space out their words/letters are fiercely independent. They place a huge premium on their freedom and do not fancy being overwhelmed by other people's values and opinions.

Letter Shape

Observe the shape of a person's letter to deconstruct their personality. People who write in a more rounded and loopy manner tend to be high on imagination, innovation, artistic prowess, and creativity. Straight, pointed letters indicate an aggressive personality and high intelligence. The person is deep thinking and

Chapter Two: Eye Movements and Facial Expressions

rational. If the letters are strung together, the individual may be orderly organized and methodical.

Analyzing Individual Letters

The way people construct individual letters reveals a lot about their subconscious thoughts and personality. There are multiple ways of writing a single letter of the alphabet, and each person has their own unique way of writing these letters, which offer wonderful insights into their persona.

For instance, dotting the lower case "i" extremely high is a sign of a free-spirited, independent thinking and creative individual. These individuals tend to be more organized and particular about details. If the dot is in the form of a circle, there are high chances that the person is more childlike and thinks out of the box. Observe closely how people construct their uppercase "I" to know their view about themselves. Is it the same size as the rest of the letters, bigger or smaller? A person who writes a huge uppercase "I" is more often than not overconfident, egoistic and cocky. If the "I" is about the same size as the other letters or smaller, they may be self-assured and happy being who they are.

Notice how people construct their lower case "t" to gather clues into their personality. If they cross the "t" with a fairly long line, it can reveal determination, passion, and enthusiasm. On the other hand, a terse cross across "t" may indicate apathy, lack of interest and low determination. People who cross their "t" high possess a high sense of self-worth and have fairly ambitious goals, while folks who cross their "t" low may be suffering from low self-esteem and may lack ambition.

If the loop in lower case "e" is narrower, the individual is likely to be suspicious or doubtful towards other people. There is some skepticism in them that prevents them from trusting people. These folks tend to be more guarded, reticent and stoic. A wide loop reveals that the individual is more accepting of different people, perspectives, and experiences. They are open to exposing themselves to new ideas and beliefs.

Next, if a person constructs their "o" to reveal a wide, open circle, they are more often than not open individuals who are expressive and don't

Chapter Two: Eye Movements and Facial Expressions

hesitate to share their secrets about their life. On the other hand, a more closed "o" can be a sign of someone who fiercely guards their privacy and is more reserved by nature.

Cursive Letters

Cursive writing can offer clues that printed or regular writing may sometimes miss, which means if you want a more comprehensive reading you should consider both.

Consider how people write the lower case "I" to know more about the person. If there's a narrower loop in the letter, it can be a signal of stress owing to limiting oneself. Similarly, a wide loop indicates that the person is not very structured or doesn't go by a set of rules. They are more relaxed, laidback and easy going.

Look the way a person constructs their cursive "y" to gather more about his or her personality. The length and breadth of "y" can be very revealing. A skinnier or thinner "y" may indicate a person who is choosy about his or her friends, while a thicker "y" represents them being more open about associating with different types of people. These people love to surround themselves with lots of friends and social acquaintances.

Similarly, a long "y" indicates a love for travel, explorations, and adventures, while a shorter cursive "y" may reflect a need to seek the familiar comfort of their home, and people they are comfortable with.

A more rounded "s" indicates a person's need to keep their loved ones happy and cheerful. They seldom engage in arguments or confrontations, and generally, maintain a positive atmosphere wherever they go. A more pointed "s" reveals a personality that is laborious, ambitious and inquisitive about ideas. Notice how the cursive "s" sometimes widens at the lower end.

This is a sign that the writer may be dissatisfied with their current job, relationship or life. They may not be pursuing what their heart genuinely desires.

Page Margins

Do people leave spaces near the edges or do they write all around the margin? Someone who leaves a huge gap on the page's left side may live in the past. Similarly, a person who leaves a

Chapter Two: Eye Movements and Facial Expressions

large space on the right-hand side of the margin may be anxious about the future. People who write everywhere on the page possess a mind racing with thoughts and ideas.

Signature

Professional graphologists can tell a lot about a person simply by looking at his or her signature. An illegible or incomprehensible signature is a sign of a person who doesn't like to reveal too much about himself or herself. They closely guard their privacy and may tend to be reserved. On the other hand, a prominent, legible signature is a sign of a person who is confident, self-assured, open and content.

Notice how some people only scrawl in the name of signature? It can indicate that the person is always in a hurry, impatient and wants to do several things at a time. Similarly, a carefully crafted and neat signature is a sign of a person who is independent, meticulous, organized and precise.

Signatures that end with an upward stroke reveal a personality that is confident, ambitious and loves challenges. They aren't afraid to dream and chase seemingly impossible dreams. Likewise, signatures that end with a downward stroke indicate a personality that is low on ambition, self-esteem, and self-confidence. These people are more likely to be overwhelmed by challenges and may not be very goal driven.

Slanting Letters

Some people write with a clear left or right side slant, while others keep their letters flawlessly straight. When a person bends towards the right-hand side, they may be easy going, congenial, open to new experiences and eager to associate with new people.

Similarly, people whose letters tend to slant towards the left-hand side are most likely introverts who enjoy their solidarity. They prefer to remain anonymous while letting others grab the limelight. An upright handwriting reflects the logical, level-headed, and even-tempered person who is ambivalent by nature.

Now, there is small pointer here to avoid misreading people. The above-mentioned analysis is exactly the opposite if you are analyzing a left-handed person. If a left-handed individual slants their letters to the right, they

Chapter Two: Eye Movements and Facial Expressions

tend to be shy and reserved introverts. Similarly, if they slant their letters to the left, they may be more outgoing extroverts.

Writing Pressure

The intensity of pressure with which a person writes can also reveal a lot about his or her personality. If the handwriting is too dark or written with intense pressure (you'll spot indentation on the back or next page), the person may be volatile, aggressive and stubborn. He or she may not be too accepting of ideas or beliefs that do not match his or her own ideas.

On the other hand, people who write with little pressure or intensity may be more empathetic and sensitive to the needs of others. They may also be more compassionate but may lack energy, enthusiasm, passion, intensity, and liveliness.

Writing That Stands Out

Look out for writing that stands out from the rest of the document. For instance, if the text is otherwise written in a more spaced out and large writing, with only some parts rammed together, it can be a sign of uncertainty or dishonesty.

Summing It Up

While studying someone's handwriting can offer a reasonably accurate insight about an individual's personality, it isn't 100% foolproof (much like every other people analyzing technique). It has its own limitations and flaws. Sometimes people tend to write in a hurry, which can change their writing. Similarly, the way people write a job application letter may differ from the way they write a love letter.

If you want an accurate analysis of an individual's personality, look at different personality reading methods such as reading their body language or verbal communication patterns. Combining different technique will offer you a more comprehensive, in-depth and accurate insight of the person's fundamental personality.

Chapter Four:
Tips For Unlocking Insights about Other People's Values

Mind reading is no magic. It is a science and skill that is painstakingly mastered by a majority of successful people in the world. Being able to read people is a gift that comes handy just about anywhere from approaching your boss for a raise to understanding your client's needs to asking someone out for a date.

Here are some tips for decoding people's values and desires through their cognitive thoughts and actions.

8. Begin With Generational Differences

Though this may not come across as a very accurate technique for decoding a person's values, it can act as a good baseline for understanding the glasses through which a particular person perceives life. Generational differences can be more intriguing than we believe.

While millennials may often believe in impersonal, non-face-to-face communication and believe in articulating their thoughts through blogs or social media, boomers may prefer person, face to face interactions. Identifying the generation a person belongs to can be helpful while approaching an individual or establishing a relationship with him or her.

For instance, if you are looking to seal a deal with a millennial CEO, you'll know that there are fewer chances of him or her wanting to finish all the formalities in person. They are someone who moves with time and will be comfortable sending documents back and forth via email. A virtual presentation may work just fine for them. However, if the CEO is a baby boomer, he or she will prefer the old-fashioned 'spending money and taking potential associates for lunch or dinner' route. Identifying an individual's generation can offer several insights into his or her values.

9. Watch People's Hot Buttons

What are the emotional triggers for a person you want to study? What does their comfort zone comprise of? Knowing people's emotional

Chapter Four: Tips For Unlocking Insights about Other People's Values

triggers can offer a good insight into their value system and desires.

My favorite tip is to learn more about people's values by asking open-ended questions. Rather than sticking to yes/no questions, try and ask questions that will elicit in-depth answers, which act as a window for the person's values.

10. Power

The manner in which people handle power or treat people who aren't as powerful as them, reveals a lot about their values or character. What is a person's attitude towards people who he or she perceives to be 'beneath' them? How does the person treat waiters at a restaurant or a customer service advisor? What is their attitude towards children and animals?

The way a person treats someone who can do absolutely nothing in return for him or her speaks volumes about his or her values. Are they particularly rude to people below their level of power? Do they engage in selfless acts? All these reveal a person's true color.

11. Reaction to Criticism

The manner in which a person reacts to criticism reveals a lot about his or her values. How does a person react to being criticized? Do they get into a fit of rage and lash out at the person criticizing them or do they coolly accept the criticism and work hard to improve on their weaknesses? Someone who handles criticism gracefully is more self-assured, confident and frank. They are not egoistic and desire to actively work on their flaws.

Similarly, people who snap on being criticized may suffer from issues related to self-confidence and self-esteem. They may need constant reinforcement of the fact that they are the best and nothing they ever do can be wrong (ego massage). These folks may suffer from a false sense of self-importance or self-entitlement. They also tend to be more egoistic. You may have to handle their fragile ego tactfully.

12. Look At The Person's Social Circle

This is no secret and has been around from the days of "man is known by the company he keeps." One of the best ways for gaining insights into a person's values and desires is through his

Chapter Four: Tips For Unlocking Insights about Other People's Values

social circle. Is he or she with the same set of friends since several years? Are they influencers within their social circle or do they lurk in the background? What are the types of people they dislike and avoid?

When I want to know more about a person's values, I always ask them the type of people they keep away from. It gives me a fairly good idea about the ideologies which clash with their own. For instance, when people tell me they don't like to associate with people who are too frivolous or partying all the time, I know these are the guys who are hard-working and goal-oriented. They are ambitious and want to accomplish something in life.

There will be something common in all the people they dislike. This trait will reveal their values. For instance, I noticed that one of my co-workers vehemently despised some people working with us. On closer observation and understanding of their personalities, I realized that all of them had one thing in common. They were all poor listeners who did not care about other people's feelings, thoughts, and opinions. All they did was focus on being heard without attempting to listen to people. This made me realize that the co-worker who hated them had a more empathetic personality and values and placed a high premium on listening to and understanding other people's feelings.

13. Language

A person's values, character, and desires are revealed to a large extent by his or choice of words. According to psychology experts, we tend to focus more on the adjectives we use than pronouns, which makes them subconscious indicators of an individual's personality. When people don't pay too much attention to their pronoun usage, they unveil a lot through it. A large number of personal pronouns indicate an egocentric or self-centered personality. It can also represent high honesty and integrity. It can also be a sign of high self-awareness or someone who is totally clued into their strengths and weaknesses.

There are many other factors such as if a person tries to use big or fancy words to make his or her point, they have a deep desire to impress others or be accepted. The person may have faced rejection or lack of attention during their childhood, which has caused them to develop

Chapter Four: Tips For Unlocking Insights about Other People's Values

feelings of low self-esteem. Similarly, people using simple words may be to the point, rational individuals who don't seek attention and are more self-assured or confident.

People who tend to use words such "except," "without" "but" etc. may most likely be honest and genuine as truthful individuals don't hesitate to offer details.

People who are happy and content don't tend to use "I" very often. Also, individuals who use the word "she," "he" "them" and "they" tend to be more focused on other people and relationships.

Even the type of jokes a person narrates or shares can reveal a lot about his or her values, attitude or character.

14. Manner in Which Someone Spends Their Money and Time

How a person spends his or her time and money is a huge indicator of their values, attitude towards life and personality. Time and money are precious commodities for people and how people spend these valuable resources can offer useful insights into their character.

Do they spend a lot of time and money on recreation activities? Do they invest time and money in building a future for themselves and their loved ones? Do they focus on learning, education, and classes? What are their hobbies and passions? Of course, I am not suggesting you go snooping around what people do with their money. All I am saying is observe how people use their finances to know their values and ideals.

15. Their Reaction to No

How do people react when someone says no to them? Are they gracious and respectful and enough to accept it? Do they react in a more volatile and violent manner? Do they respect boundaries set by others? Does the individual then go on to manipulate the decision to get a "yes" from the other person? A person's reaction to "no" can reveal volumes about how he or she is as a person.

16. Gut Feeling

You can learn all the scientific people reading techniques in the world and still rely on your instinct when it comes to reading and analyzing people. If you have a particularly bad feeling about something or someone persistently and

Chapter Four: Tips For Unlocking Insights about Other People's Values

can't pin it down to a rational thought or occurrence, it may most likely be instinct or intuition.

Though it doesn't seem like it, even our gut feeling is a deeply scientific process that is closely linked to the limbic brain. It is merely responding to subconscious clues that our conscious mind hasn't caught yet. If you get a feeling that a person is not right for you, your gut feeling may be right!

Chapter Five:
Rebranding Yourself Using Body Language

While meeting people for the first time, we're all eager to make a killer first impression. There is an undisputed eagerness to say and do all the right things at the right time. Much as you'd like to believe that everything you say is making an impression on you, what you are leaving unsaid also says a lot about you.

Nonverbal communication (including body language, gestures, and tone of one's voice) plays an equally important role when it comes to rebranding yourself or wowing people. You can say everything you want to verbally but still not leave the desired impression because your body language is not making a wow impression or isn't compatible with what you are verbally expressing.

Even people who aren't trained to read people through body language can subconsciously latch on to signals that your nonverbal communication or body language gives.

Here are some tips for creating the perfect impression with body language.

17. Keep a Relaxed Posture

Stand straight in a relaxed and easy position but don't lighten up so much that you look too casual or nervous. The worst you can do is sport a slouching posture. Make sure to be mindful, purposeful and conscious of your posture now and then. A hunched back is a sign of being nonchalant or nervous/unsure about a situation. When you keep your posture upright in a more relaxed manner, you not just look confident but also feel more confident subconsciously.

Firm Handshake

A firm handshake is a sign of self-assuredness, confidence and high self-esteem. With a firm grip, you give the impression that you are totally in control of yourself and everything around you. You'll get added points for making direct eye contact and smiling while shaking hands with a person for the first time. It shows you are

Chapter Five: Rebranding Yourself Using Body Language

genuinely pleased to meet the person and are interested in what they have to say.

Be careful of keeping the handshake firm and not crushing his or her hand or you'll come across as increasingly aggressive, and he or she may subconsciously dislike you immediately. You want to come across as confident and in control not overbearing.

A weak, limp and listless handshake, on the other hand, can signify an uncertain, nervous and inhibited personality. It reveals a timid persona and lack of self-confidence.

Mirroring the Person's Actions

Man is wired since primitive times to show affiliation towards another human through mirroring his or her actions. It is so deeply embedded in the subconscious mind that we don't even realize it is happening.

Now that you know it, use this information to your advantage. When you mirror people's actions, they form a subconscious connection with you, and view you as "one of their kind." The result, they end up forming a favorable impression of you or liking you almost immediately.

The act of mirroring should be gradual and discreet, not very obvious or the person will think you are mimicking them, which will be counterproductive. If the person is leaning against the bar while speaking to you, you do the same slowly. If they raise their glass to take a sip of the drink, follow suit. If they move their weight from one leg to another, gradually attain the same posture.

Look at the way they are using their hands. What are the gestures they make frequently? What are the typical words and phrases used by them? Try to mirror their gestures, expressions, and words. Match the tone of the voice. What is the typical manner in which they speak? Do they speak in a restrained, hush –hush tone? Or are they loud and enthusiastic while speaking? Observe all this and try to incorporate as much of their verbal and nonverbal patterns as possible without making it too obvious.

Body language experts suggest aligning your body with the body of the person you are communicating with. Position your body to face

Chapter Five: Rebranding Yourself Using Body Language

him or her directly. This reveals your interest in engaging with him or her or giving them your complete attention, which everyone appreciates.

If the person you want to make a favorable impression on is standing in a group, and it isn't possible to directly face him or her, don't try to cut people off or leave them out of the conversation.

Rather, pivot your attention strategically towards the person you want to impress by making frequent eye contact with him or her (even while addressing the group), and offering a friendly smile. Don't stop a conversation and move your body towards him or her when in a group. It will only make you look eager to impress and overbearing.

Keep Legs and Arms Uncrossed

This may not be important when you are communicating casually with a close friend or family members. However, it holds plenty of importance when you are communicating with someone for the first time and want to create a stellar first impression. Like we discussed earlier, it is a defensive position. People will view you as guarded, closed and secretive. You are less likely to come across as a genuine, open and honest person. Crossing arms and legs can also be a signal of disinterest (pray don't do it on a first date or that all important client negotiation) or absolute boredom.

Proxemics

Use proxemics to your advantage by maintaining appropriate physical space between you and the person you want to impress. Proxemics is nothing but the study of physical space when it comes to nonverbal communication.

Psychologists and body language experts believe that the amount of physical space a person leaves while interacting with another person reveals a lot about the dynamics of their relationship or the equation between the two. When you are meeting a person for the first time and trying to make a favorable impression, do not try to invade their personal space.

Maintain a minimum distance of four feet between with him or her as a rule of the thumb until you get to know them better. You can demonstrate your interest by leaning slightly in the direction of the person but don't attempt to

Chapter Five: Rebranding Yourself Using Body Language

get too physically close to them too soon. Even if you aren't leaning ahead, ensure that you don't lean behind. Just maintain a steady, relaxed and upright posture. Leaning back can signify lack of interest or boredom.

Small Talk Does Big Magic

Verbal exchange plays a huge role in determining the impression you create on a person. Learn something about the person before you meet them or attempt to strike a conversation with them. Digging a little into their background on the social media will give you a good idea about their likes, dislikes, hobbies, professional, etc.

Does he or she volunteer at a community organization? Do they play golf? What are the things you have in common with this person? These are good starting points for making a meaningful and engaging conversation.

One of my favorite tips for making a favorable first impression on people through small talk is going through the entire newspaper or browsing the net for the day's most happening news stories. If nothing else works, you can start by making a conversation about world events. This will make you come across as an engaging and well-informed conversationalist.

Just ensure that you don't share your views or opinion on something controversial, religious or political and you'll do fine. Stick to general, non-controversial topics such as new discoveries, path-breaking research, advancement in technology, weather, global economy, etc. Small talk indeed goes a long mile when it comes to making a favorable first impression.

Show Attentiveness and Courtesy

I'll let you in on a secret. One of the best ways to be instantly likable and desirable to people is to listen to them. And listening doesn't mean having your ear in their direction. It means giving them your undivided attention and acknowledging what they are saying.

You can offer plenty of verbal and nonverbal clues that you are keenly listening to the person in the form of nodding your head, verbally acknowledging what he or she is saying and paraphrasing their sentences to show you are closely listening to what they are saying.

Chapter Five: Rebranding Yourself Using Body Language

Do not, I repeat, do not keep looking at your phone or pretend to be distracted. If you want to make a favorable impression on the person, give him or her undivided attention, demonstrate good manners and be polite/courteous towards everyone around. Mirror the other person's actions naturally.

Chapter Six:
Reading People through Their Words

The eyes may very well be the windows to a person's mind and soul, but their words reveal how they think, process information or offer insights into their character. Words represent both thoughts and feelings. Listening to a person's words can reveal a lot about his or her inner thoughts and ideas. Specific words can indicate the behavioral traits of a person who said or wrote them. These are words clues that help you predict the person's characteristics almost accurately. Though you may not be able to read their entire personality through words, you get a good idea about the behavioral patterns and thought the process of a person.

Our brain is nothing short of a marvel. While thinking, we tend to use more of nouns and verbs. On the other hand, when we try to express these thoughts in spoken or written form, we emphasize on adjectives and adverbs.

The basic structure of a sentence comprises a verb and subject such as "I ate." Any more words that are added to the subject (I) and verb (ate) can offer clues into the individual's behavioral characteristics. Any words added to a basic sentence help you make educated guesses about the person. For example, if a person says he or she walked briskly, it can indicate a sense of urgency. They may walk briskly or quickly, owing to their need to be on time for an appointment, which demonstrates a more conscientious mindset.

People may also walk quickly out of fear or when there is a threat. It can be a threat in a potentially dangerous neighborhood or bad weather. When someone uses the word quickly, watch out for more clues about why he or she has chosen to use that particular word. Here are some pointers to read people through their word clues.

18. I worked really hard to accomplish my dreams

The word hard here suggests that the person loves to chase goals that are challenging to accomplish and doesn't like anything that comes

Chapter Six: Reading People through Their Words

easy. It can also be an indication that the particular goal he or she is referring to was particularly tough compared to the ones he or she achieved earlier. Using words such as "hard" also reflect a mindset that is ready to postpone gratification to accomplish his or her long-term goals. He or she most likely holds the view that dedication, perseverance and hard work is the key to producing stellar results.

At times, people convey a lot through what they leave unsaid.

Let us try understanding this with an example.

You are a server at one of the plushiest fine dining restaurants in your city. It serves multi-course meals that are much sought after by patrons. You have a family over at the restaurant for a multi-course meal one evening, and warmly welcome them. As a server, you introduce them to each course and offer interesting trivia behind each of the preparations, keeping them enthralled. You are sure they've had a wonderful time and enjoyed their meal. When they've paid the check and are about to walk out, you ask them if they liked the food. The man says, "The soup was good!" You aren't pleased. Why? Did he say the soup was good right? What do you think is the reason for your disappointment?

The answer lies in focusing on what he left unsaid. When the man said the soup was nice, he indirectly implied that the rest of the food or other courses weren't as good as the soup or were average. They were nothing to talk about. This is precisely the reason why we sometimes get offended when someone looks surprised and says, "you are looking good today." What they leave unsaid is, you don't normally look this good every day. Thus, while people convey a lot through the words they use, they also communicate a lot through the words they leave unsaid.

I made up my mind to buy that home

If a person says he or she has decided to do something or made up his or her mind to something often, they may have considered many options before arriving at a decision. It means the person may be more contemplative and take his or her time to weight his or her options before concluding. They deliberate upon their decisions and are more analytical by nature. There are very slim chances of him or her

Chapter Six: Reading People through Their Words

being a rash or impulsive decision maker. These are more signs of an introvert than extrovert personality.

However don't be quick to jump to conclusions as soon as someone uses the word "decided." Look for a pattern and other clues that point to a more reflective, thinking and introvert personality. A definitive personality assessment needs thorough psychological observation and assessment, and making sweeping conclusions about people based on a few words will only land you in trouble.

Extroverts gather their energies from others and seek greater environmental stimulation. They tend to use the trial and error method rather than deliberating upon a decision. Introverts will rarely speak without thinking, while extroverts tend to be more spontaneous.

It helps if you know beforehand whether a person is an introvert or extrovert to mold your communication pattern according to their predominant personality. For instance, if you are a salesperson, knowing whether your prospective client is an introvert or extrovert will help you determine how he or she makes decisions.

Introverts take time to mull over things and make up their mind. Similarly, if you are negotiating an important business deal, it is important to understand if the other person displays characteristic of an introvert or extrovert.

If you notice a predominantly introverted mindset, give them more time to think before they take a decision. Pushing them into making a quick decision may go against you (they will most likely respond in the negative if they aren't given enough time to consider their decision).

On the other hand, a person who shows signs of making quick decisions may be an extrovert. These people can be goaded into taking fast decisions and actions. They can be pressurized into making instant decisions because they are more comfortable doing things without thinking excessively about them. However, one of the most important considerations is that people rarely exhibit a completely introvert or extrovert personality. Most people are a combination of both. They like to be around other people but also value personal time and space.

Chapter Six: Reading People through Their Words

Uses of words such as "right" and "wrong" often

Notice how people often say things such as "I did the right or wrong thing." These words suggest a strong inclination towards ethics and morals. It reveals that they may have overcome an ethical dilemma that helped them make a just or unjust decision, which has either made them happy or disillusioned. Using the word "right" all the time demonstrates a strong character and the need to be ethical. They most likely make the right judgment even when there is a conflict or when they are confronted with an opposing view.

When you tune in carefully to people's words and listen to what he or she is saying, their words can reveal a lot.

I sat patiently through his or her talks

Like we discussed earlier, the adverbs a person uses in a basic sentence helps describe his or her state of mind, thoughts or feelings. For instance, if the person is said to have patiently listened to someone, it means he or she wasn't making much sense or that they were boring. Perhaps the person had to attend to nature's call and still sat patiently through someone's talk.

Irrespective of the reason of why he or she said that it implies that they were preoccupied with another thing. This is an individual who listens to social etiquettes and customs, while not offending established norms.

If you are interviewing someone for job recruitment purposes, this may most likely be your ideal candidate who respects authority, establishments and rules.

Talking about others

Haven't we all heard that all famous quote about how what we say about us reveals plenty about us?

In a study conducted by Peter Harms at the University of Nebraska, and Siminie Vazire at the Washington University in St. Louis (published in the Journal of Personality and Social Psychology) it was found that simply by asking a group of participants to rate negative and positive characteristics of three people helped researchers understand the each participant's mental health, overall well-being, social attitude and the way they were perceived by others.

Chapter Six: Reading People through Their Words

It was found that a person's tendency to see others in a more positive light was a reflection of his or her own positive personality traits. He or she viewed others pretty much with the same filters that he or she used for themselves. There was a strong co-relation between judging others in a positive light and being happy, enthusiastic, courteous, compassionate, emotionally stable and able themselves. Talking about other people is positive, encouraging words is a huge sign of how overall satisfied people are with their lives, and how they are viewed by other people around them.

Conversely, negative words used to describe others are highly linked with antisocial behavior, overall dissatisfaction with their life, narcissism, and a low sense of self-worth. People with predominantly negative traits tend to view and speak to others in a negative or unflattering manner. It can also be an indicator of personality disorders or mental health issues.

Chapter Seven: Reading People through Their Environment

A person's immediate environment can reveal a lot about his or her, and I don't mean the pop psychology quizzes that keep pooping on your timeline. I mean it is a solid, scientific way to make educated guesses about a person's character. There are psychological principles behind analyzing a person's behavior through his or her immediate environment.

Here are a bunch of awesome, proven tips for reading a person through his or her surroundings.

19. Colors

The first thing you notice when you enter someone's home is the colors used in the décor. A person's choice of colors can psychologically reveal several aspects of their personality. For instance, if the person is using a lot of bright, bold colors such as red, orange, electric blue, etc., he or she is unafraid to take risks or articulating their thoughts. Their personality is bolder, outgoing and adventure bitten. They are not afraid to say things as they see it.

Subtle colors may imply that the person is more subtle, restrained and reflective in nature. They may be deep thinkers who weigh all options carefully before taking an important decision.

People who are more focused inwards or introverts tend to do up their homes on solid, soft hues and more muted patterns, while outgoing personalities tend to use bold, experimental designs.

The Hidden Closet

The mess in your house probably reveals the mess in your head too! No, that's not being judgmental. It is a way to analyze how people's thoughts and mind leads to the creation of their environment. A neat, organized, efficiently categorized work desk is a sign of a mind that possess great clarity of thought. Excessive cleanliness or orderliness can also be a sign of anxiety, nervousness or low self-esteem. It can also point to a mental health issue such as obsessive-compulsive disorder. Watch out for

Chapter Seven: Reading People through Their Environment

signs of extreme orderliness and an obsession with cleanliness.

On the contrary, people whose spaces are more chaotic and disorganized looking can reveal a cluttered and disorganized mind. It can be a sign of being good at many things or multitasking. When you are engaged in too many activities, you barely have the time to organize your space, which means it is often left unattended or in a disorganized manner. Sometimes, it can be a sign of plain laziness or lack of clarity/objectives in life.

It has been observed that people with a more extrovert personality tend to have more chaos around them. Their drawers will most likely be messy and disorganized. On the contrary, people who are more reflective and introvert by nature will spend more time meticulously organizing, arranging and prioritizing their belongings.

A majority of people (however picky about cleanliness) have some areas of the home that are a hidden mess. Think under the bed or behind their closets. These are mostly areas that are not often accessed by people and therefore neglected. If a person keeps even these inaccessible areas neat and organized, they may be suffering from anxiety. These are the most likely the type of people who are control freaks or are obsessed with being completely in control of everything around them.

Studies also reveal that a messy, disorganized and erratic environment is a sign of high creativity. People living in such places tend to generate better and more path-breaking ideas. So yes, the cliché about an artist of scientist/inventor with messy hair and a disorganized look is actually true from the psychological perspective.

Prints

Amusing as it sounds, I can tell a lot about a person simply by looking at the prints they use in their décor or on their clothes. Big, bright and bold prints reveal that the person is more self-assured, confident and not inhibited by other's opinion of him or her. They are most likely fiercely independent in thought and action, and original thinkers. They have their own clear opinion/views on several issues and aren't easily influenced by others.

Chapter Seven: Reading People through Their Environment

Similarly, quirky prints such as polka dots or animals or comic legends can reveal a fun, whimsical, creative and original personality. Geometric prints, on the other hand, reveal a need for order and organization.

A study conducted by researchers at Yale concluded that people who spend a long time on showers and bathing are mostly lonely. They use the warmth of the bath as a substitute for the lack of emotional warmth.

Psychologists have also deciphered the meaning of having a wall filled with motivational quotes, messages, and posters. According to experts, this is most likely an indicator of neuroticism. These folks use their immediate environment to soothe their nerves and help them sail through. Don't immediately conclude something is wrong with a person or that he/she needs help if they have a wall full of motivational posters. Talk to them more to gain a better understanding of their personality or observe them closely to gather non-verbal clues.

Old Items

People whose spaces are filled with items from the past such as old job uniforms, sports team jerseys that no longer fit, clothes that they've outgrown, etc. are the ones who most likely live in the past or are unable to let go of their past. They cling to memories and often refuse to move on. Hoarding things belonging to their past is not a sign that they are attached to the belongings per se. These people are in fact clinging to the memories associated with these belongings.

Chapter Eight:
Determining Personality through Birth Order

Analyzing people through their birth order isn't just a bunch of stereotypes or cocktail party talk but a fairly accurate manner of predicting someone's personality based on their childhood experiences. Our birth order often determines the roles we play in our families or the status quo we are given during our early childhood years, which ultimately shapes our fundamental personality or the way we relate to others.

Even though it seems like a study in pop psychology, subconsciously the way we relate to our immediate family members during early childhood has a deep impact on the way we turn out as adults. Many parents will vehemently confirm the fact that each of the children is different from the other regarding personality, though they are all raised in the same house/environment.

There are several factors that along with birth order determine the personality of an individual, and these factors are so closely woven that they cannot be isolated while studying an individual's personality of his or her birth order. Some of these factors are: number of family members or children in the family, the family's socioeconomic status, the parent's education level, environmental factors, and more.

Alfred Adler (an associate of Sigmund Freud and Carl Jung) was the first to propose the theory of determining an individual's personality through his or her birth order while analyzing his clients. However, it was psychologist Frank Sulloway of MIT who modernized the theory for contemporary application.

In his path-breaking book, Born to Rebel Sulloway named five primary traits that defined a person, which are extraversion, neuroticism, openness, agreeableness, and consciousness. According to him, a person's birth order impacted all these fundamental traits. He made a startling conclusion that people who have the same birth order have more in common personality-wise than siblings who are raised together. This is because, according to him, a

Chapter Eight: Determining Personality through Birth Order

person's birth-rank impacts them more than his or her environment.

According to author and parenting expert Grose, two children never assume the same role within a family. We all automatically and instinctively take on roles within groups without realizing it. Our families are often the first group we are exposed to. The dynamics that define the role we take on in the very first group largely influence our personality.

Here are a few tips for reading people through their birth order.

20. First Born

The stereotype of firstborn individuals is that they are natural leaders, ambitious by nature and innately responsible. This is partly true because for some time the child doesn't have any competition when it comes to earning the affection and attention of family members. They don't have to compete with siblings for time and attention from parents. This gives them a slight edge over siblings.

Again, they tend to be caretakers or surrogate parents for their younger siblings (often teaching them things the older child has learned before, the younger siblings). This makes them develop leadership skills and a more accountable, responsible nature. They are protective by nature, and often lead the way for others.

On the flipside, if parents place great expectations on the firstborn, and he or she feels incapable of matching up to those expectations, they can develop a damaging personality that is marked by low self-esteem, the constant need for validation and acceptance from others, low self-confidence and a general feeling of never being good enough for anything or anyone.

According to Sulloway's research, firstborn showed more signs of conformism for rules and respect for authority/tradition. They demonstrate signs of respecting the established status quo rather than challenging it.

A study about firstborns reveals that they tend to be more goal-oriented and place high importance on success and accomplishments. Their place in the birth order makes them lean towards achievements. The first born's

Chapter Eight: Determining Personality through Birth Order

personality may also be marked by a constant need to be control and authority, at times making them appear bossy or dogmatic. They are almost always concerned about other's approval.

As per Sulloway's birth order theory, firstborns who are considerably physically stronger than their younger siblings are likely to demonstrate dominant behavioral traits.

Some typical traits of first-born people are – goal oriented, responsible, determined, conformists and meticulous/detail oriented.

Middle Borns

Middle borns often have a more complex personality because they don't enjoy the special rights of the oldest child nor the leeway or privileges of the youngest child. They are awkwardly juxtaposed between the two, owing to which they turn out to be excellent negotiators or peacemakers. These are also people who have a wider social circle as they rely on friends for attention and support when parents focus more on the youngest or oldest sibling.

In case the oldest child doesn't fit the role of a leader at home, the middle child takes his or her place or fills their shoes. Also, there can, in fact, be several middle children. How does one determine their personality in such a scenario? For example, in a family of five children, there can be three middle children. As a rule of the thumb, each child shows personality traits that are different from the one immediately next to him or her in order. This means that within the three middle children, the first and last will have more similar traits than the middle one.

Middleborns are typically social by nature and are obsessed by a sense of fairness and peace. They are known for their excellent negotiation skills, which make them good diplomats and peacemakers.

While the oldest child enjoys undivided attention from parents, while the youngest can get away with murder, family's middle baby is often left with neither. Since they are literally juxtaposed in the middle, they turn out to be amazing compromisers, peacemakers, and negotiators. These kids are harder to pin down and are more loyal, faithful and relationship-oriented by

Chapter Eight: Determining Personality through Birth Order

nature. They seldom let down people who trust them or are close to them.

Middle borns typically display these personality traits – they are peacemakers, flexible, accommodating, diplomatic, free-spirited and magnanimous. They are known to work well in teams and relate well with people who are younger or older to them in age or authority since they have a more amiable nature. Middleborns are also known to be competent in more than a single skill.

Last Born

The last born is often known to be a charmer and risk taker. They are more free-spirited, creative and adventurous. There is a tendency to reinvent the wheel rather than following established rules and norms.

Parents tend to be less careful and cautious with the last born since they've already lived through the experience of being a parent at least once and aren't as overwhelmed by the prospect as when they became parents for the first time. Also, parents generally tend to be more financially well off than they were during the birth of the first child, which means there is a tendency to indulge the child more.

Parents are more relaxed when it comes to following rules, which means the youngest child doesn't develop traits of a conformist. They are used to being pampered and showered by attention. Since parents are more lenient with youngest borns, they don't tend to be very rule oriented or revere established authority. There is a tendency to make their own rules, and create new paths rather than walking commonly walked paths.

Typical personality traits revealed by last borns are rebelliousness, empathy, creativity, high sense of self-worth or self-esteem and stubborn. The youngest child often displays traits related to attention-seeking, sociability, extroversion, and manipulativeness. They make for great sales professionals and know how to get their way around people.

A study conducted in 2001 revealed that last-born children show an inclination for careers related to creative arts, and the outdoors. On the contrary, firstborns show an inclination for intellectual vocations.

Chapter Eight: Determining Personality through Birth Order

Only Child

Now, again, the stereotype about an only child being self-centered or creative is not entirely without a strong reason. Since they spend a lot of time in solitary activities, they tend to be creative, entertaining and innovative. They always find resourceful ways to keep themselves busy, earning self-entertainment skills.

Much like first-borns who get used to having their parents' undivided attention until their siblings are born, only children are often self-assured, confident, meticulous and articulate. Since only children don't have to compete with siblings for their parents' attention or material belongings, they tend to develop a sense of self-entitlement and self-centeredness.

They get used to having things their way and find it challenging to cope when things do not happen as they desire. Firstborns always want to be the important people around and have a hard time sharing the limelight with others. Another most marked trait about only child is they are perfectionists. Owing to the fact that their only role models are their parents or other adults in the family, they tend to become huge perfectionists.

21. Factors That Make the Reading More Accurate

There are many factors influencing an individual's personality that can make your reading more accurate. Psychologists often suggest looking at a person's siblings while analyzing his or her personality since two children within the family rarely share the same role. You will know the role played by the individual you wish to analyze by observing his or her siblings.

Some other factors affecting your reading are genetics and gender. A majority of our personality is determined by gender and genetics in addition to the birth order, which means these are also factors worth considering while analyzing a person's birth order.

Conclusion

Thank you for downloading the book, How To Analyze People: *21 Fundamental Techniques to Interpret Body Language, Personality Types, Human Psychology and Secretly Analyze People.*

I sincerely hope it has offered you several valuable insights into reading people's personality through proven strategies, tried and tested subconscious techniques and a treasure trove of practical tips. These tips can be applied just anywhere, in any situation from business to interpersonal relationships to social settings to negotiations.

Whether you want to figure out the personality of a potentially big client during a negotiation or the characteristics of the hot new prospective date you have your eyes on, this book is a handy resource for helping you read others effectively. If there's a single largest skill that spells success in today's world, it is the ability to read people.

This allows you to mold your message according to the personality of the other person to accomplish optimally beneficial communication.

The next step is to use the book and apply it in your daily life in small, gradual ways to begin with. Start by observing people at the airport or doctor's clinic when you have some time at hand. The interest will quickly catch on, and you'll find yourself taking a deep interest in reading and analyzing people.

Lastly, if you enjoyed reading the book, please take the time to share your views by posting a review on Amazon. It'd be greatly appreciated!

Manipulation

----- ❦❧ -----

How to Secretly Persuade, Emotionally Influence and Manipulate Anyone Including Spotting Mind Control Tricks

David T Abbots

Table of Contents

Introduction 99

Chapter One: Manipulation and Mind Control Techniques..109

Chapter Two: Emotional Manipulation Techniques 133

Chapter Three: The Body Language of Manipulation 151

Chapter Four: Reading Body Language and Analyzing People.. 165

Chapter Five: Secret Social and Subconscious Manipulation Strategies 183

Conclusion 189

Introduction

Manipulation is primarily the art of getting people to do precisely what you want them to do without focusing on their needs and desires, and in extreme cases, even causing them harm. However, though manipulation has majorly negative undertones, it can be used for persuading and influencing people. It can consist of a series of techniques like charisma, trickery, misinformation, hypnotism, and wordplay.

The prime objective of manipulation is to trick people into doing what you want them to do without them realizing that they are being manipulated or being led into doing something. Sometimes, manipulation can be used to accomplish a positive outcome by turning the game when nothing else seems to be working.

For example, let's say you are due for a promotion and pay hike after working hard for your organization, but the firm just won't relent. When logical and other straight techniques don't

Manipulation

work, you may have to resort to manipulation to get your stingy employers to give you your due. In such situations, manipulation is used constructively to accomplish a positive goal when you can't break through another person's unreasonableness or stubbornness.

Knowingly or unknowingly, we've been practicing manipulation even before we started speaking. Babies want to be fed, kept clean, and put to sleep. Toddlers cry for toys until the parents give in. As an adolescent, we manipulate people to go on dates with us.

Manipulation originates from the primary belief that your requirements or desires come before everyone else's. For the manipulator, the world revolves around their needs and desires. However, manipulation can be lent a more positive angle when it is used to align you and other people's needs.

Unlike persuasion or influence, manipulation happens at a more subconscious level. It is done to change an individual's primary beliefs, feelings, and experiences for getting them to do what you want. It can be accomplished by using a range of techniques from verbal and non-

Introduction

verbal communication to hypnotism to smooth seduction techniques. Manipulation is essentially distorting an individual's perception of reality. The manipulator gets people to think in the direction he/she wants to.

If you've read Shakespeare's tragedies such as Othello or Macbeth, manipulation forms the central theme of their plot. The ingenious playwright understood manipulation in relationships, politics, and leadership even before there was a popular term for it.

In Othello, the villain Iago employs a bunch of vicious psychological tricks, including deception and craftily planned scenarios to get Othello to suspect his trusted chief

lieutenant Cassio so Iago can replace him. Lago creates a complex plot that leads Othello to believe that his ladylove Desdemona is cheating on him with the lieutenant. The villain uses his knowledge of psychology to climb his way into power by manipulating people's thoughts and circumstances to suit his quest for power.

Macbeth is another popular Shakespearean tragedy that is based on the theme of

Manipulation

manipulation. Lady Macbeth manipulates her husband using several psychological techniques to eliminate King Duncan and proclaim himself the ruler of the mighty Scottish throne. Macbeth then goes on a murderous rampage to protect himself from suspicion and enmity, which presents him a tyrant. The bloodbath ultimately led to the downfall and end of Macbeth and Lady Macbeth.

Lady Macbeth and the witch sisters use a series of manipulation strategies throughout the classic to instigate and encourage Macbeth into performing inhuman acts that eventually led to his doom. They manipulated Macbeth into thinking that he alone is capable of ruling the land, thus planting seeds of ambition, power, and hatred, which caused his and Lady Macbeth's end.

Is it possible to manipulate constructively or positively?

Yes, manipulation can be used positively and negatively depending on the end result—think about manipulating a perennially depressed person into seeing a counselor after failing to persuade him/her through other means. Then,

Introduction

imagine manipulating a drug addict or alcoholic into giving up the substance or alcohol. That isn't too bad, is it? You are using supposedly negative techniques to accomplish a positive goal.

Positive manipulation or persuasion/influence has been going on for ages. Religious leaders, political bigwigs, and social reformers attracted people like magnets through manipulation with their positive energy, ideas of humanity, equality, and brotherhood. That wouldn't qualify as tricky manipulation. They influenced people with their positive ideas, personalities, and examples to learn important life lessons.

There are multiple times in your life when you've wanted to transform someone's life for good. Yet, people may turn down your straight attempts to reach out to them owing to many reasons. In such cases, persuading or influencing people through the use of trickery or manipulation to fulfill a positive end for their own benefit may not be so bad. Irrespective of the techniques you use, your tactics cannot be termed devious or crafty.

Sometimes desperate times do indeed call for desperate measures. Using straightforward approaches may not work all the time. The only way you can get someone to do something is by using backhand techniques. Your objective isn't to get the person to do what you want to fulfill a personal agenda. It is to move past a person's stubbornness and obstinacy.

Let us consider an example to see how manipulation can be used positively. You have a childhood buddy Ray whose wife has just left him for another man. Predictably, it has turned his life on its head. The two of you have been thick since childhood before Ray moved to another city for work. You get to know through a mutual friend that Ray has gone into severe depression, which has affected not just his personal life but also his work. His performance at work is abysmally down, and he could lose his job soon. Since you are old friends and concerned about Ray, you are worried about his depression and the subsequent effect it is having on his work.

You are aware that he is a primarily emotional, sensitive and psychologically weak person who wouldn't have taken this development very kindly. Like any good old childhood friend, you go over to meet Ray and talk to him about it. He shares his story with you, and you suggest he see a counselor.

Ray is adamant that he won't visit a counselor because he doesn't see how it can help bring back his wife, whom he loved dearly. You try to reason with him and tell him that it is not about getting his wife back. Rather, it is about getting a grip on his life and moving on. Again, he refuses to budge. He just doesn't understand how visiting a therapist or counselor can resolve his problem. His life is going more and more downhill with every passing day, and you just can't see him in letting his life slip away from his hands in this manner. You try to coerce, persuade, and convince him using every trick in the book, but he doesn't buy it!

How do you overcome this obstinacy and unreasonableness?

In absolute desperation, you tell him how your co-worker's wife left him, and he went into severe depression. You go on to list details about how the unfortunate event affected his performance at work. As a manipulator, you pick the right words, gestures, expressions, voice, theatrics, and emotions to let your friend know

Manipulation

that the co-worker really had a tough time coping with his depression. You launch into overdrive describing how it consumed his personal and professional life.

This is the point where you slowly introduce the idea of how your co-worker decided enough is enough and that he was going to take control of his life by seeking professional help. You booked an appointment for the co-worker with a counselor, and on your recommendation/suggestion, the co-worker agreed to see the counselor.

With the practiced tact of a manipulator, you inform Ray about how the co-worker's strong will and multiple beneficial counseling sessions helped him slowly to get his life back on track. You inform him going for regular therapy, and counseling sessions gave your co-worker the hope and courage to tackle the seemingly adverse situation in his life. What you are doing is stirring the right emotions within the person to get him to act in his best interests while moving past his unreasonableness and stubbornness.

Introduction

You are hoping that after hearing your co-worker's story, Ray is also moved into taking action. After listening to the story, Ray decides to see a counselor and starts going for regular therapy sessions. Slowly yet surely, you can see his life getting back on track. Ray appears more in control of his life, and his performance at work starts improving.

Here's the catch, my friends. None of what you told Ray is true. It is a cleverly spun tale and fabricated instance involving an imaginary co-worker. It involves lies, misinformation, and deception. However, is making up a story or manipulation in such a scenario so bad? You made it all up to push Ray into taking action. You manipulated your friend Ray into meeting a counselor and helped him move on. The aim is to enhance his psychological condition through trickery, manipulation, and lies. Sometimes, manipulation opens a small window through which an individual moves past his stubbornness to take action in the right direction.

Even when you are training an animal to "sit," "fetch," "jump," etc., by dangling their favorite treat, you are actually manipulating them to do what you want them to. Yes, it may be referred to as training, but that's just a clever play of semantics. You may be training your dog to stay out of harm or lead a more disciplined life, which may be positive manipulation.

If you are a parent or have ever observed one, you know it is a herculean task to get kids to do something against their will. Parents are perpetually offering made up stories about angels, fairies, Santa Claus, monsters, and more to get them to do things that are good for them (the kids). Well, eating spinach doesn't give you superpowers, but sometimes that's the only way to get a stubborn toddler to eat it.

Subtle manipulation can be used for motivating and inspiring people for doing things that are good for them. Utilizing these approaches, you can transform someone's self-image, addiction, bad habits and more.

Think of manipulation as a work tool like a hammer. It can be used to hit a nail on the wall, or it can be used to destroy the wall. It is like holding a matchstick in your hand. You can light a candle for light, or you can start destruction by causing a fire.

Chapter One: Manipulation and Mind Control Techniques

Before we begin discussing ways to manipulate people by using mind control techniques, bear in mind that, on the whole, manipulation isn't considered a good way to accomplish a goal. Instead of using this mental trickery to fulfill evil personal agenda, use it for a positive purpose or to detect manipulation in your daily interactions. Protect yourself from manipulative folks and get people to accomplish more positive goals by applying these powerful persuasion/manipulation techniques.

World renowned social psychologist Robert B. Cialdini has mentioned six primary principles to change people's thoughts, feelings, and actions that, when practiced, help you become a powerful influencer and persuader.

Manipulation

1. Reciprocity

People have an innate need to return another person's favor. When someone buys you an expensive gift, you feel obliged to return an equally expensive gift or a valuable favor. If you want to get a person to do something, bring about a feeling of obligation in them. Keep reinforcing everything that you've been doing for a person over a period of time. Say something like, "Oh! Wouldn't you do the same for me or help me when needed?" in place of "Oh! It is nothing; please don't embarrass me by mentioning it." You are subtly planting the idea that in the future, you expect them to reciprocate by doing what you want.

2. Scarcity

When something is scarce, we tend to value it even more. This is a popular manipulation technique used by advertisers, marketers, and brand managers to get consumers to buy their products. Think "limited edition," "while stocks last," "limited period offer," "selected customers only," and more. When you position something as scarce, rare, or available for only a limited period, people tend to act with a greater sense of urgency and take immediate action.

3. Commitment and Consistency

Get people to do what you want them to do by getting them to commit. It is simpler to persuade them into doing what you want. For example, if you get someone to give something in writing or make a public declaration about their intention to do something, they can be held responsible or accountable for failing to do it. This increases your chances of getting them to do what you want them to do. People don't like going back on their words or being seen as someone who doesn't live up to their commitments.

4. Authority

Ever wondered why a majority of health, hygiene, and safety product promotions and advertisements have "authorities" or "experts" in a field waxing eloquent about how buyers will benefit from buying these products? Social media influencers get paid handsomely to promote products and services in the form of reviews or recommendations. People dig authority and expertise. If they view someone as an authoritative expert in a field, they are likelier to do what he/she tells them to do. If you want people to take a specific action, bring on board someone who they view as an authority. Get the expert to tell them what you want them to do. It works! Again, whether these methods are utilized to fulfill a negative or positive outcome is up to the person using them.

5. Liking

Answer this honestly. A very attractive, confident and friendly salesperson in a store is selling the same thing that another plain and slightly hesitant salesperson is selling in another store. Who will you purchase from? Though both are nice people, you will buy it from the person you like, and—correct me if I am wrong—a majority of people will like a person who comes across as attractive, charismatic, and friendly. Spend more time with a person to increase familiarity. Instead of asking your crush straight out for a date, get them to like you by hanging out as pals. There are fewer chances of a person refusing because you are now familiar with them, and they like you.

Chapter One: Manipulation and Mind Control Techniques

6. Social Proof

Whether you see this as a bane or a boon, people are wired to do what everyone else is doing. The herd mentality is deeply ingrained in the human mind since our hunting/gathering era. People invariably assume that because everyone is doing something, it must be the right thing to do. How many times have you been invited to a social gathering only to inquire who will be in attendance? There are higher chances of you attending when you realize everyone from your circle of friends, co-workers, or competitors are going to be there. There is a deep-seated fear of being left out. Why do companies and businesses ask for reviews from existing customers to attract new customers? Social validation!

18 Powerful Strategies for Manipulating People

We practice manipulation in some form or another throughout our lives, though its magnitude varies vastly. There are plenty of sneaky techniques, strategies and tricks to control people's minds and get them to do what you want.

Manipulation

How can you control another person's mind by bringing about a shift in their subconscious mind? Here are some powerful tips to control other people's thoughts, feelings, and actions without making them realize that they are being manipulated.

1. Establish Similarity

People instantly take to people who they perceive to be similar to them. It dates back to the primitive times when humans communicated their similarity with each other or being one among the same group through non-verbal communication. Establishing similarity works effectively until today. When you are trying to get people to do what you want or impress them, focus on creating familiarity.

People will develop a powerful sense of affiliation if you demonstrate that you are one among them through your voice, choice of words, and body language. This will increase your chances of getting them to do what you desire.

If you are trying to win over someone you've just met (a potential client or date), mirror their actions. Carefully notice the way they walk, talk,

Chapter One: Manipulation and Mind Control Techniques

hold their glass, lean against the bar and more to follow suit. Try using the same words and expressions they use. Observe the way they hold their glass. Sip on your drink a few seconds after they sip on theirs. If they shift their weight from one foot to another or lean against the wall in a specific manner, follow suit. Mirror their intonation, words, expressions, gestures, and posture.

Make the mirroring subtle and inconspicuous. The act shouldn't be too noticeable, or it may backfire, and the other person may think you are making fun of them. Mimicking can be offensive to the other person, and it'll only end up hurting your cause. This works especially well in a professional scenario where emotions rarely work.

2. Develop Charm and Charisma

Charisma is hard to explain but can be instantly identified in people when seen. Charm and charisma can help you impress people in a smooth/effortless manner to do what you want them to. They can seamlessly work their way into hypnotizing people with their charisma to think, speak, and act in a specific manner.

Manipulation

Practice developing a warm, inviting and congenial vibe. Stay approachable, friendly, and humorous (especially self-deprecating humor that makes you come across as more confident). Keep your body language open and flexible (more on manipulating people through body language later). Work on your conversation skills, appearance, and oratory skills to win people over. You should grab people's attention and arrest their interest through slick conversation skills. Learn the art of making small talk to establish a killer rapport with people.

People who are experts in manipulation almost always have excellent conversational skills. They will compliment people lavishly to win them over or make them feel exclusive/special. They'll look people in the eyes while talking with the intention of influencing people. If you want to manipulate a person into doing what you want, make them feel special. Give them the feeling that you are truly interested in their feelings, desires, and emotions. Demonstrate that you are going out of your way to understand them and care for their interests even if you don't actually care.

Chapter One: Manipulation and Mind Control Techniques

Confidence is another big attribute of charisma. Seasoned manipulators often have magnetic personalities and know the effect they wield over people. Confidence makes people more attractive. It reveals to the other person that you know what you are saying, which makes you more persuasive and believable. If you have complete faith in your abilities, you will be likelier to succeed when it comes to influencing people to think/behave like you or in another specific manner.

When people notice your confidence, they place greater trust and faith in you. They will take your actions seriously when they realize you know precisely what you are saying or doing. This comes only by practicing confidence. Be smooth talking and glib when you want to get people to do what you want, irrespective of whether you are speaking the truth.

3. Take Drama or Theater Lessons

One of the greater challenges when it comes to manipulating people is to master the right emotions, expressions, intonation, voice, words, and body language when you may not be feeling it. You are contriving or faking a specific set of actions to get the desired result.

You may have to pretend being distressed, unhappy, or disillusioned when you don't have your way to persuade people into giving in to your demands. Taking drama or theatre lessons is a clever way to sharpen your manipulation skills.

Master manipulators know how to master their emotions. Practice controlling your emotions and actions while trying to get people to do what you want. You may have to cry or appear elated in seconds. You'll have to learn to put up various acts according to the situational demands. Mastering the art of using your emotions, expressions, and actions at will is a valuable skill for any manipulator. Note: don't let people you are intending to manipulate know that you are taking acting lessons or your acts won't have much credibility or authenticity.

4. Practice Reading and Analyzing People

Every person has a unique personality, which means the same manipulation techniques may not work for everyone. You'll have to use distinct

Chapter One: Manipulation and Mind Control Techniques

emotional, psychological, and logical techniques to get people to respond in a specific manner based on their personalities.

Identify people's hot buttons or trigger points before attempting to manipulate them (much like the way salespersons do). What is their fundamental personality? How do they think, act, feel, and behave? What are their inherent desires, fears, and motivators? Take time to analyze people's personality before manipulating them. What moves them or makes them tick? Which is the best approach to get them to do what you want?

Identify people who are receptive to emotional responses, who are easier manipulation targets. Psychologically it is easy to manipulate people who display more emotional responses such as sympathy for other people, empathizing with other's problems, feeling disturbed when others are hurt, crying while watching sad movies, feeling a sense of compassion for animals and more. To get these people to do what you want, you have to awaken their emotions psychologically.

Manipulation

Similarly, other people are more prone to logical responses and therefore will respond more favorably to facts, figures, statistics, and other hard data. When you observe that a person keeps up with news reports, facts, and figures before making important decisions, use a more rational, persuasive, and composed approach. A calm and logical approach can work effectively when it comes to influencing people. Use a more calm, subtle, and logical approach that doesn't involve excessive use of emotions.

5. Fear-Relief Technique

This is a highly proven manipulation tactic that you've probably used knowingly or unknowingly at some juncture. Follow up an unreasonable request with a more realistic request to increase your chances of getting the other person to agree with you. This works at a deeply psychological level where the person places both the requests against each other and feels slightly relieved by the second request after being disturbed by the initial unreasonable one.

The feelings of confusion and tension are thwarted by the second request, thus increasing

Chapter One: Manipulation and Mind Control Techniques

your chances of getting someone to agree to your actual request.

Let us say for instance you want to seek permission from your boss to leave work early for the next couple of days. You ask your manager for permission to leave early for the next few months. When he/she appears taken aback by the idea, you immediately claim the opportunity to say something like, "Hey, Peter, no stress. Would you please allow me to leave early for the next couple of days?"

He/she will be relieved because this seems like a more reasonable request compared to the first one. The person will be more receptive to your request. Also, once he/she has refused something, it is more challenging to follow it up with another negative answer. The person will most likely relent to your request.

Fear-and-relief is a wicked psychological manipulative technique which works like a charm. It is considered essentially evil because it involves preying on an individual's emotions by causing him/her a great deal of anxiety and then abruptly relieving that built-up stress. The person becomes disarmed after the rise and drop

Manipulation

in emotions, which makes him/her less prone to make logical decisions. Thus, they are more likely to respond more positively to your request.

Here's a study that demonstrated how fear-relief works wonders when it comes to manipulating people.

These experiments listed in The Science of Social Influence and Will demonstrate how fear-relief manipulation works on a subtle level to accomplish the desired results. In one of the experiments, mall visitors were alarmed by a stranger who suddenly tapped them on their shoulder from behind. When people turned around, they found a blind man who wanted to know the time. After the fear and relief, the blind man's associates ask their targets to purchase and sign postcards for charitable causes. The rollercoaster of emotions got the targets to do things more effectively than control group participants who didn't go through the fear-relief manipulation.

The classic technique is evident in the bad-cop, good-cop routine. An authority scares the wits out of you, and another comes over and rescues you. Thus you become more open to sharing

Chapter One: Manipulation and Mind Control Techniques

information. Insurance salespersons use the technique all the time, and so do crafty managers. They will scare the shit out of you by informing you that your job is in jeopardy. Then, they'll request you to put in additional hours of overtime if you want to save your job.

6. Get Your Foot in the Door

The foot-in-the-door strategy was used by door-to-door salespersons in olden times when they tried to put their foot in the door to prevent people from banging the door on their faces. Today, the technique is used for establishing a rapport with people or breaking the ice by making a small request that is easy for them to fulfill. Later, you move in with the bigger and actual request very subtly. What you are doing is launching a series of positive replies.

This technique is the opposite of the earlier manipulation strategy. It is based on the psychological principle that once a person replies in the affirmative to your tiny and reasonable request, it will be tough for them to reply in the negative for what you actually want them to do.

7. Use Home Turf Advantage

When you are planning to get someone to do exactly what you want them to, arrange to meet on home ground to gain a clear psychological authority or advantage over them. When a physical space belongs to you, you subconsciously wield more control or authority in the situation.

It can be any place where you exercise greater psychological dominance (home, workplace, vehicle, etc.) to any other place where you feel a sense of familiarity, belongingness, and ownership. The other person should experience a sense of being on unfamiliar ground so they can rely on your confidence to make their decision.

This is exactly why friends and acquaintances who plan to sign you up for network marketing businesses will also ask you to join them for a presentation at their place or territory that is familiar to them over a space that belongs to you. They rely on the home ground advantage to get you to agree to their schemes and proposals.

Also, if you are negotiating a big business deal or getting a prospective client to agree to purchase

Chapter One: Manipulation and Mind Control Techniques

your products or services, it may work to your advantage if you get them to agree to come over to your workplace or a restaurant that is familiar to you (or where everyone from the server to the owners knows you well). What you are doing is giving yourself a psychological edge by negotiating on familiar ground.

8. Bribe

The powerful strategy of rewarding a person with the intention of getting them to return the favor can work well across situations. Reward a person psychologically, emotionally, or materially with something, so they feel compelled to return the obligation. When they do return the obligation, make sure it is by doing what you want them to.

Start by recognizing what your boss or partner wants, and do it for them. Don't forget to make it clear to them that you are doing them a favor, and when the time comes, you expect it to be returned. When you want them to do something for you, strike and remind them that it is time to give back.

While using this mind control or manipulation strategy, don't let it come across as emotional blackmail or it'll backfire. The idea is not to let the other person know that you are manipulating them into acting in a particular way. Let it come across as you are genuinely trying to help the other person by going out of your way. This technique works well because the other person perceives a clear benefit initially and hence feels persuaded to give in.

For example, if you plan to ask your manager for a few days off work, prepare in advance to put in a few extra hours before asking him/her, especially if it's a busy time and he/she is likely to refuse your leave application. Stay up late and ensure he/she knows that you are going beyond your call of duty to fulfill the need of the hour. Subtly follow it up with your request of taking off from work for a few days. It is almost impossible for someone to refuse!

9. Use the setting to your advantage

Use the environment to your advantage by asking a person to do something for you at a place where they won't expect you to ask for it. Thus, you catch them off guard and disarm them before getting them to agree to your request. Don't be too caught up with "there is a place and time for everything." Make the setting work in your favor by coming up with an unusual request.

For example, let's say you are out at the bar with your co-workers after work. Instead of asking for a favor in the office, use the chilled out and leisurely setting of the bar (when people are likelier to be in a more relaxed state) to get the person to agree to your request. When people are in a good mood or relaxed state of mind, they are less likely to refuse your requests. Go for the kill in a setting that is different from the expected setting to boost your chances of getting a positive response from the other person.

10. Gaslighting

Gaslighting has been extensively used in movies and books as a popular manipulation technique. It is a covert manipulation technique where a manipulator twists reality to meet their agenda. It is comprised of misleading the other person to believe (irrespective of whether it is their fault) that it is indeed their fault that they aren't able to perceive reality correctly.

The notion that they aren't able to see things correctly becomes so deeply embedded in their mind that they begin to question their perceptions and instead accept the manipulator's version of reality or truth. The technique is one of the most dangerous forms of manipulation because it is about making the other person feel so mentally incompetent that they stop having faith in themselves. It goes to the extent where they become mistrustful of people who oppose their perceptions because the ideas are so deeply sown in their psyche.

11. Rationalization

Rationalization is another effective technique through which a manipulator cleverly justifies their downright hurtful or inappropriate action. The technique works well because the justification offered is logical enough for a person to subscribe to it.

Rationalization accomplishes three primary purposes including removing resistance that manipulators may have about their not-so-appropriate acts, preventing other people from pointing fingers at them and assisting the

Chapter One: Manipulation and Mind Control Techniques

manipulator in justifying their actions in the eyes of the victim.

Manipulators who utilize the power of rationalization generally behave in a very affectionate manner. Suddenly, they'll become cold, hard, and distant. The victim is soon exhausted by their behavior, and when he or she confronts them or avoids them, they will start crying or screaming and launch into overdrive about how stressed, upset, and depressed they have been lately. The manipulator makes the other person feel miserable about confronting them when they are clearly not in the right frame of mind.

The other person, not you, becomes the bad person when someone confronts you for your inappropriate behavior. The victim becomes the insensitive person instead of you. Manipulators move people to tears with how stressful and tough their life really is. They are adept at playing the victim and even justifying their terrible actions by blaming it on other people through rationalization rather than accepting the blame for their actions.

Manipulation

12. Master Your Own Emotions Before Preying on Other People's Feelings

This is last but certainly not the least. To be a class act manipulator, you have to have complete control over your feelings and emotions. You have to make people like you by coming across as positive and friendly all the time. As a manipulator or persuader, you will be required to get people to think, feel and act in a certain way. This requires you to be completely in control of your emotions.

You cannot be swayed by your emotions if you are aiming to control someone else's feelings. If you don't learn to master your emotions, you may end up being manipulated instead of manipulating others. Avoid falling into the plan you create for others and aim to create fear, uncertainty, or sympathy in others while being completely in control of your own feelings and emotions.

Manipulation is all about controlling and directing other people's feelings and emotions in a specific manner. Manipulators are compelled to exercise control over a situation to covertly or openly control other people's thoughts, feelings,

Chapter One: Manipulation and Mind Control Techniques

and actions. For example, you will make someone believe that they are overreacting to a situation when they are clearly not. Controlling other people's actions, feelings, and thoughts becomes easier when you are control of your own thought patterns and emotions.

Chapter Two: Emotional Manipulation Techniques

I think we've all forgotten how many times we've been told if we love someone we'll do things their way (read: go to a specific place to eat or go to the games over movies). Yes, that is the potency of raw emotions. It can be used constructively and destructively to get people to do what we want them to. Emotional manipulation happens when you leverage other people's feelings and emotions to your advantage or to accomplish an overall good. Again, it's a double-edged sword that can be used to fulfill some positive and negative intentions.

Here are some powerful emotional manipulation techniques:

Playing on People's Fears

Emotional manipulators tend to exaggerate facts or selectively highlight facts/reality/statistics to induce a sense of fear in their victims. For instance, a person who doesn't want their partner to pursue a full-time career outside their home and raise children instead may say something along the lines that, "research reveals 70 percent of all relationships break up when both partners pursue full-time jobs."

There can be other reasons too, but the manipulator chooses to create fear or a sense of insecurity by highlighting a single aspect to get their partner to act in a specific manner. This helps them play on the other person's fears that if they indeed give in to their ambition, they may end up losing the relationship.

Make the Other Person Feel Guilty

A majority of emotional manipulation techniques involve stirring a sense of guilt within the other person. Practiced manipulators know how to make the other person feel guilty to fulfill their own agenda. For instance, if someone brings up a grievance that is bothering them for a while, emotional manipulators will make them feel guilty for even making an issue out of a non-issue.

Chapter Two: Emotional Manipulation Techniques

Again, if they don't speak, emotional manipulators will make them feel guilty about hiding their feelings or not having a frank, straightforward conversation. As a manipulator, you keep brewing guilt in the other person irrespective of their thoughts and actions. Anything the other person does is attributed to them, so they are overcome by a strong sense of guilt and finally give in to your demands. Building a sense of guilt is one of the most powerful ways to get a person to obey you.

This works even more effectively on people who are not very sure of themselves or possess low self-confidence/self-esteem or are essentially indecisive. For example, if you want to get a friend to do exactly what you want, list everything you've done to help them, followed immediately by a mention of the times they've completely let you down.

You can also stir up an overpowering feeling of guilt within your partner by saying things such as, "it is okay, one can't expect anything different from you." This makes them feel like they are letting you down all the time, and that you can't expect anything else from them.

Manipulation

Observe how some seniors induce a strong sense of guilt in their children by emphasizing the fact that they (the children) don't spend time with their parents despite knowing that they aren't going to live for long. The children may be busy with their own hectic schedules and make time whenever possible.

Similarly, if parents don't allow their teenagers to go on a camp or a night out with friends, the adolescents will make their parents feel guilty for being overprotective and not allowing them to negotiate the world on their own. We use emotional manipulation in several ways throughout our lives. Only the intention and intensity varies from person to person.

I am sure you know someone who plays victim all the time even if life isn't as hard as they imagine it to be. These people will use their helplessness to act like victims and make others feel guilty to get them to do what they (the guilt-trippers) want. They give others a feeling that their fate is often in other people's hands. The other person then feels responsible for them, which induces a deep sense of guilt. They feel terribly guilty about refusing this person because the manipulator has craftily presented

Chapter Two: Emotional Manipulation Techniques

themselves as someone who needs help, and who'll be completely lost if you don't help them. The other person will invariably feel bad and do exactly what you want them to because they start feeling responsible for your fate and sense of helplessness.

Challenge the Other Person's Sense of Reality

Emotional manipulation also involves challenging or belittling the person's understanding of reality. Manipulators are skilled liars and deceivers. They possess the ability to confidently tell someone that something happened even though it may not have happened and something didn't happen when it may have happened. They can change someone's perception of reality by playing around with facts in a sneaky manner.

The victim of their manipulation will begin questioning their own perception of reality or sanity. For instance, if someone suspects the manipulator of having an affair and questions them about it, the manipulator will not only deny it but also turn the game around by making the other person feel guilty about doubting them.

Manipulation

They'll make the other person come across as crazy, suspicious, insecure, and possessive, owing to which the person may start questioning their own sanity or sense of reality.

Play The Victim

Seasoned manipulators put on the victim's garb with ease. If you plan to manipulate people emotionally, one of the most powerful ways is to act like a victim or behave like it is never your fault. Irrespective of who is at fault, manipulators will always blame their actions or shortcomings on others.

Focus on how someone made you do something even though you didn't necessarily want to do it. If the manipulator is hurt, upset or angry, the other person is blamed for hurting them. In short, manipulators do not accept any accountability from their actions.

Let us consider an example; If a regular person forgets their anniversary and the partner gets upset, he/she will apologize profusely to the partner and attempt to make up for it by doing something special for the partner.

Chapter Two: Emotional Manipulation Techniques

However, a manipulator will not just fail to accept their mistake, they will, in turn, make the partner feel guilty about blaming them for such a trivial matter when they've been stressed at work and have tons of things to remember. I know of people who will go even beyond that and remind the partner about all the instances where they've forgotten important things as a justification for their blunder.

One-upmanship

One-upmanship games are common among manipulators. Irrespective of how big other people's challenges and problems are, as a manipulator, your challenges and problems should always be pitched as worse. The idea is to undermine the genuineness of another person's problems by constantly playing up your issues as greater than theirs.

You make other people feel guilty for complaining about non-existing issues when you are fighting bigger battles. The idea is to make the other person feel like they don't have a reason to complain, while it is your right to focus on your rather "serious" issues. You want the other person to stop complaining and stay one-up during every situation, even when it comes to playing the victim.

Know Their Emotional Hot Buttons

One of the best ways of emotionally manipulating people is to know their emotional triggers or hot buttons. Everyone has their weak spots that can be used to get them to do what we want. Manipulation is about identifying these weak spots and using them to your advantage to get the person to do what you want.

For instance, if you know that a person is unsure or slightly conscious about their appearance, play on their insecurity by passing remarks about their weight, clothes, or appearance. Again, if someone is not confident about their public speaking or presentation skills, play on this fear by informing them about how difficult and judgmental the listeners are. Use the awareness of other people's emotions to get them to do what you want by leveraging them smartly.

Induce an Inferiority Complex

Emotional manipulators engage in decreasing a person's sense of self-worth or undermine their

Chapter Two: Emotional Manipulation Techniques

belief in themselves by judging, analyzing or criticizing the person. The objective is to marginalize, ridicule or dismiss a person constantly in an attempt to gain a sort of psychological dominance over them.

The objective is to make the other person feel off-balance, inferior and inadequate to get them to act in the way you want. When other people stop believing in their abilities or sanity, you have more control over their thoughts, feelings, and actions.

Emotional manipulators will intentionally plant the feeling that something isn't quite right with the other person to shake their sanity or sense of self-belief to fulfill an agenda. They'll make the victim feel like nothing they ever do is going to be enough. Importantly, the emotional manipulator will concentrate on the victim's weaknesses without offering positive feedback or constructive solutions, and guide them to overcome their weakness in meaningful ways.

The Silent Treatment

Another powerful manipulation weapon is the silent treatment. Emotional manipulators have mastered the art of giving people the silent treatment to pressure people into doing what they want. They will purposefully make a person wait and plant seeds of doubt and uncertainty within the person's mind. Emotional manipulators utilize the power of silence to keep their victims emotionally unsure or deprived.

The silent treatment can be used as a tool to encourage people into doing what you want them to do. You refuse to acknowledge their existence or make them feel inadequate to accomplish your objectives. If the victim's actions do not match that of the manipulator, the manipulator can convey their disappointment by penalizing the victim with the silent treatment.

Use Humor to Disempower People

Emotional manipulators use the power of humor to pick on people's perceived limitations or weaknesses in an attempt to disempower them or make them feel inadequate. Have you ever noticed how sometimes people make critical or caustic remarks about their friends or family in the disguise of humor? The objective is to make the other person feel insecure or inadequate.

Chapter Two: Emotional Manipulation Techniques

Emotional manipulators aim to throw their victims off guard by playing on their limitations and weaknesses. The remarks may appear humorous on the face of it and can target anything from the individual's appearance to their abilities to their smartphone. They may make fun of anything from the fact that you walked in late to the clothes you are wearing—with a clear intention of throwing you off balance or making you feel miserable about yourself.

This is a way to gain a psychological edge over the other person by undermining their sense of self-worth. The person starts feeling inferior, which disempowers them on a subconscious level and makes them more open to control or dominance.

Flattery

This almost always works like a charm if you do it right. Flattering words and compliments have the potential to move anyone's heart, but the intentions behind those words may not always be noble. Flattery is a weapon of attack for several manipulators to persuade people into fulfilling their personal agenda. As a tool of manipulation, flattery is used magnificently well by salespersons. To make this even more effective, make your compliments specific.

For example, rather than saying "your presentation was really good today," say, "I loved the ease with which you handled objections" or "I loved your closing statements." Specific compliments hit the nail on the head. For example, let us say you are in an apparel store trying something that you think doesn't look too good on you. However, the salesperson walks in and says, "Wow blue is indeed your color, this looks fabulous on you." What is your reaction? Don't you feel influenced to buy it immediately? There is a quick shift in your thought process. Flattery is a sneaky little trick to sweep others off their feet and get them to do what you want.

Ignorance or Helplessness

Helplessness and ignorance is another powerful tool used by manipulators to persuade people into doing what they want. You'll feign or pretend that you are not able to do things and use helplessness as an emotional manipulation trick to win other people's sympathy.

Chapter Two: Emotional Manipulation Techniques

Sometimes, use the excuse "you're better than me" or "smarter than me" to get someone to do something for you. However, ensure that you don't use this tactic frequently or people will see through your game.

Create a Sense of Urgency and Alarm

"Sale ends today" or "if you can't make a decision today, I am not staying here anymore" are typical phrases used by manipulators to get people to act by creating a sense of urgency. They may create a fake sense of panic or urgency to push people into taking action. When people feel like they don't have much time or they'll miss out on something important if they don't take action, their chances of doing something increases.

Use People's Commitments and Promises against Them

Who doesn't fancy being a "man of their word" by sticking to what they say? However, manipulators will cleverly use this trick to get people to do what they want by using their words against them. Life keeps changing, and people's promises keep fluctuating. However, if you are a smart manipulator, you will know how to use people's commitments and words to get them to do what you want. Even though things may have changed and it isn't possible to do what people earlier stated, use their words as an emotional manipulation tactic to get them to do what you want. Bring up their promise several times to let people know that they've got to do what they promised or they run the risk of being seen as someone who doesn't live up to their word or commitment.

Overcome trust issues

If someone has been manipulated several times before, they will most likely not trust people again. If trust is a major issue, nix it by sharing something private and personal with your target. It is all the more effective if the secret is relevant to the person or if they perceive that you trust them enough to share something so personal with them. Whether the story is true or not is irrelevant. You are focusing on winning the person's trust by demonstrating your faith in them. Again, putting on act is the clinching factor.

Chapter Two: Emotional Manipulation Techniques

Sugarcoat negative manipulation as altruism

Approach everything in a friendly and positive manner. Negativity doesn't make you an efficient manipulator. The key is to come across as a wonderful person who cares about others. Negative actions such as blaming, criticizing and yelling at another person should always be sugarcoated with altruism. Painting yourself as an altruistic person saves you from acquiring the label of a manipulator. People seldom despise someone who claims to care for them and wants the best for them.

For example, let us say you feel the need to yell at the other person for not taking an action you asked them to take. If you frame this as something you wanted them to do, you'll run the risk of coming across as selfish, self-centered, manipulative, etc. However, if you present the same thing as a way of helping them, the other person will feel you are acting in their interest.

Let us say as a boss, you give your employee some additional work to complete back home during the weekend which you were supposed to complete during the week. The employee didn't

Manipulation

finish it, and if you felt the need to yell at him/her for not getting your work done, you will naturally come across as selfish or self-centered. However, if you present it as something that will affect the employee's appraisals, reviews, chances of promotions, etc., you come across as a hero who cares about the employee's professional success and wants him/her to perform well or impress the management. Thus you are sugarcoating your own selfish desires as altruism.

If you are prone to outbursts, you'll have to learn to get a good grip on your emotions. Manipulation and emotional outbursts do not go well together. It may help you in a few instances, but in the long run, positive manipulation is more effective than negative manipulation techniques. If you do give in to an outburst, apologize to the person by stating that you were overcome by emotions because you care about him/her or are acting in their best interests. Never fail to remind the target that you will always be there for them.

Chapter Two: Emotional Manipulation Techniques

Act normal when you are caught manipulating

Several newbie manipulators falter when it comes to responding when their manipulative acts are discovered. When someone calls out your manipulative actions, the most terrible thing to do is engage in a more manipulative behavior. Stay normal or composed when someone calls out to your behavior.

Allow the other person to control the situation while you stay passive. Avoid defending your actions. The sole way to wriggle out of the situation is to stir doubt and make this doubt work to your benefit in the minds of your victims. Appear genuinely shocked and revolted. Create a shocked expression and make the other person feel guilty about their assumption. In a majority of the cases, people will start questioning their own assumptions, especially if you are well-known to them. They will latch on to any reason to believe in your positive virtues.

Learn More About Psychology and Neuroscience

Know more about psychology, human behavior, and neuroscience to manipulate people more effectively. You should have a fundamental understanding of how people think and behave if you desire to be a powerful manipulator. Sure, all the tips mentioned here are going to make you an effective manipulator, but you need a deeper understanding of human psychology to know which manipulation principles to apply in which situation, and to manipulate people effortlessly.

Chapter Three:
The Body Language of Manipulation

Manipulation is about persuading people to do what you want them to, which involves plenty of people influencing skills. Non-verbal communication comprises expressions, gestures, posture, walk, leg movements, voice, tone, etc. and is responsible for a major part of the communication process.

According to research conducted by Dr. Albert Mehrabian, only 7 percent of our communication happens through words. About 55 percent of the entire communication happens through body language and 38 percent through our voice. Now you can imagine why people insist that you meet them in person (and not over the phone) when they want to share something important with you. Body language and voice makes up a huge chunk of the communication process, which means manipulators need to master these elements to convince or persuade people to do what they want.

Manipulation

The manner in which you convey certain concepts, thoughts, emotions, facts, and feelings is going to influence other people's decisions. Communication skills are important when it comes to influencing people to do what you desire or take the required action. Hone your manipulation skills by mastering powerful communication techniques to come across as more persuasive, inspiring and influential.

Here are some secret tips to use when making non-verbal communication skills, including body language and voice for manipulating people into doing what you want them to do.

1. Let the other person talk first to establish a baseline.

When you are attempting to get someone to take a specific action (for instance: purchase from you), allow them to talk first. This way you get a chance to set a baseline for their behavior and detect their weaknesses that you can play on later. The personality or behavior baseline will give you a clear idea about thoughts, actions, motivators, needs, feelings, and behavior to help you determine their strengths, weaknesses, and goals. I'd say, go one step ahead and create a

Chapter Three: The Body Language of Manipulation

questionnaire to get the answers you are looking for.

2. Listen to people.

Manipulators must not just be excellent speakers. They must also be exceptional listeners. Practice active listening to know exactly what a person wants. It'll also give you a clear idea of a person's personality, needs, and wants. Listening to a person arms you with the power to come up with an appropriate response to what they are saying. For example, a prospective buyer or client may not need to purchase from you currently or may be considering purchasing from a competitor, and by not listening to them you are missing out on important bits of information.

If you miss this important information, you will not be able to handle their objections effectively. Since you haven't heard about their reference to a competitor, you won't be able to do a comparative analysis later to establish how your product is superior over a competitor's.

To make yourself more likable and accessible to people, acknowledge what people are saying by nodding or saying "hmms" or imitating their expression. You can also paraphrase what the person said to ensure you've heard it right. "Mr. XYZ if I get you correctly, you are not considering buying this product right now because you want to do a comparison with our competitor's prices, products, and features too? Is that correct?" Resist the urge to interrupt the other person while speaking and don't jump to offer solutions before the person finishes talking.

Even if we don't realize or admit it, all of us drift off after a point of time. Ask questions and repeat the last few words to clarify important points or give the other person the idea that you are keenly listening to or interested in them. Listen to people with an open mind without judging what they are saying.

Avoid being a conversation hijacker. Sometimes, your thinking will be quicker than the other person's pace of speech. You'll be tempted to finish their sentence for them while they are still grappling for the right words. This again does not give the other person a chance to finish what they are saying, and you may miss important bits of information. Don't listen to respond or start

Chapter Three: The Body Language of Manipulation

constructing your responses while listening. Listen to understand.

This will give you a greater edge while manipulating people. Try to remember what people say with the help of keywords or create a mental visual to better remember what they spoke.

3. Body language

Keep your body language confident, authoritative, poised, and self-assured. People buy your body language before they buy your words when they meet you for the first time. They are likelier to be taken in by a confident body language and voice. If your body language or voice is filled with hesitation or self-doubt, there's a slim chance others will accept what you are asking them to do.

- Manipulators are adept at the art of looking people in the eyes while speaking to come across as genuine and honest. While talking to people, face them and maintain eye contact all through the conversation. Constantly shifting your gaze away from the person makes appear dishonest. Again, fixating your gaze on a person makes you come across as intimidating. The best part is to look away briefly from time to time.

- A smile works wonderfully when it comes to establishing a rapport or a feeling of belongingness or similarity on a subconscious level. Boost your likability factor by having a smile plastered on your face permanently.

- Always lean slightly towards the person you are talking to. This reveals attentiveness and interest on your part. The head should be tilted towards them or in their direction while maintaining a healthy distance between the face. Point your feet towards them rather than the exit or the opposite direction!

Avoid invading a person's private space by getting too close to them physically. You should leave a gap of at least four feet between you and the other person. Just tilt your body in their direction or lean over a tabletop to reveal your interest in

Chapter Three: The Body Language of Manipulation

them while communicating/interacting with them.

- Stay attentive, unruffled, and relaxed. Avoid tapping your feet or fidgeting with your hands. It conveys the message that you are nervous or disinterested in what they are saying. Keep your feet and hands in a more relaxed position without being too conscious of it. Nervousness and manipulation/persuasion never go together.

- One super way of enhancing body language is to practice in front of a mirror. It allows you to determine how you appear to other people and what changes can be made to make your communication and presentation skills even more impactful. Notice your expressions, gestures, walk, posture and more. Do they have the intended effect on people? Do you appear calm, confident, persuasive, and self-assured while speaking? Does your speech inspire people to take immediate action?

Manipulation

When you meet someone for the first time, set your subconscious authority by offering a firm, assertive, and power-packed handshake. A limp and lifeless handshake communicates nervousness, uncertainty, and lack of confidence. It is easy for the other person to gain a psychological dominance over you, which will make it tough for you to manipulate him or her. Similarly, a crushing handshake indicates aggressiveness or absolute dominance.

- Amy Cuddy, a renowned social psychologist has mentioned a list of how to use specific power poses to your advantage in a TED Talk. The power postures will not just boost your testosterone levels but also decrease the body's cortisol levels in less than two minutes. These poses are believed to have a considerable impact on our thoughts, feelings, and actions on a very subconscious level. They give the message of the power of authority to the other person.

Chapter Three: The Body Language of Manipulation

A majority of these postures involve occupying more physical space by broadening your frame to make yourself appear powerful and bigger. When you take up greater physical space, you subconsciously establish yourself as a larger or more authoritative/dominant person.

While standing, expand your stance by keeping the feet apart. You will appear less nervous and more in control of the situation. Holding your feet together will make you come across as nervous and unsure.

- Research in the field of brain imaging has revealed that our brain's Broca area is responsible for speech stimulation within the body. This happens not just when we are talking but also while performing gestures such as moving our hands. Thus, our speech and hand gestures are more intricately woven than we realize. Thus by engaging your hands through gestures, you can facilitate your thoughts, ideas, and words.

Some of the world's best speakers move their hands in animated gestures to make an arresting impact on their listeners. Your speech, thoughts, presentation, and clarity will be significantly enhanced if you use gestures. Eventually, you'll come across as more persuasive and convincing.

- Establish a quick rapport with the other person if you want to influence him/her into doing what you want with the help of body language. Face them directly while talking and be attentive while speaking. This will align your body language with their verbal and non-verbal communication pattern, which is especially helpful while addressing a group. When you want to influence or manipulate people into doing something, it is important to align with their body language and show them you are completely attentive and attuned to them through verbal and non-verbal signals.

4. Voice

Manipulators or persuaders/influencers generally have a more relaxed voice with a low

Chapter Three: The Body Language of Manipulation

pitch and assertive tone. Always speak in a low and assertive tone to come across as more authoritative rather than talking in a squeaky, high-pitched voice. The voice shouldn't rise when the sentence ends. It reveals doubt or uncertainty. It comes across as if you are asking a question or raising a doubt about something rather than making an assertive or authoritative statement. Allow your voice to completely relax before making an important presentation.

Maintain an assertive arc that works wonderfully well when it comes to manipulating/persuading people. The voice starts on a gentle note, while the pitch rises in the middle of a sentence, and eventually cascades at the end of the sentence.

A person's voice tone reveals plenty about how a person is feeling. If you don't speak in a consistent or even tone, it comes across as if you are concealing emotions or are not in control of your emotions such as nervousness, anger, and disappointment. Know when to pause to create the intended impact. When you make a powerful statement, pause to allow the idea to sink in!

Also, emphasize the right words to create the desired effect. Emphasizing the right words lends more impact and greater clarity to your communication, which is important for getting someone to take the required action.

An animated voice along the lines of voiceover artists or radio personalities works well when it comes to lending more punch to your message. Don't speak in a flat monotone throughout a speech or conversation. Vary it by lowering or elevating the pitch for creating the desired histrionics. One tip is to listen to famous radio presenters to understand how they modulate or play with their voice to evoke the desired emotions among listeners.

Volume depends on the people you are addressing. While addressing a big audience, keep it loud and authoritative. However, if it's a one-on-one conversation, speak in a low and soft tone.

5. Appearance

An attractive and pleasant appearance adds to your likeability factor and charisma. We discussed earlier how you are likelier to purchase from a person who is more physically attractive than someone who is plain-looking. Basic

Chapter Three: The Body Language of Manipulation

hygiene is the essence of being presentable, likable, and charismatic. People who smell good attract others like magnets.

Humans are drawn to clean, well-groomed and hygienic people on a primordial level. At a fundamental level, it is easier to manipulate people if you smell good and are clean. It will be challenging to manipulate people if you stink or appear untidy or unclean. Being well-groomed and hygienic doesn't require much effort. Shower, groom your hair neatly and wear a nice smelling fragrance.

Have a neat and well-groomed haircut that suits your face. The presentation of your hair impacts your overall appearance. Your haircut or hairstyle is one of the initial things a person notices about you when you try to influence them. Dress well if you want to make a favorable impact on people and appear confident.

Wearing well-cut outfits with flattering fits will make you look good. And we all know when we look and feel good about ourselves, our confidence shoots up several fold. Looking good will make you come across as more confident, self-assured, and influential. People will be more

Manipulation

likely to look up to you and agree with what you say if you come across as confident and in control. Try taking someone whose appearance or attire you do not like seriously. It just won't click.

Chapter Four:
Reading Body Language and Analyzing People

To manipulate people, you've got to dive right into their mind and understand what they are thinking. Master manipulators are adept at the art of speed reading people through verbal and non-verbal signals. Only when you understand people are you able to determine the right approach for manipulating them. For instance, some people are more prone to emotional responses and reactions and emotional manipulation may work well for them. Similarly, others may be more logical by nature. For such people, logical manipulation techniques may work more effectively.

You can determine your own body language, words, expressions, gestures, and more to manipulate people once you know how they are thinking or feeling. Here are some of the best body language tips to read people.

Manipulation

Crossed Arms And Legs

Folded legs and arms are a nonverbal signal of a subconscious barrier. It demonstrates that the other person is psychologically closed to what you are speaking or isn't interested or trustful of what you are saying. Sometimes, they may have a smile on their face, or they may speak in a friendly manner. However, their non-verbal gestures may reveal a different story about their psychological thought process.

Crossing arms and legs is a signal of creating a physical or psychological subconscious barrier between the speaker and listener. When you get a feeling that the person is shutting off from what you are saying by crossing their hands and legs, change the topic to something that is of interest to them. Allow the other person to get into a more relaxed frame of mind or open up a bit before getting back to the original topic. The process happens so subconsciously that the other person isn't even aware of it.

Real Smiles

How can you distinguish a genuine smile from a fake one? Here's the deal. Our mouths can often

Chapter Four: Reading Body Language and Analyzing People

contrive smiles even when we don't feel like smiling. However, the eyes and the region around the eyes cannot deceive since it's a very subconscious driven microexpression.

When a person is genuinely smiling, it is evident in their eyes. A real smile reaches the eye and causes the skin around the eyes to form wrinkles or crow's feet. People fake smiles to hide their true feelings. However, seasoned manipulators will look for crinkles near the eye region to determine if the person is indeed happy or simply faking delight.

Eyes Don't Lie

When people don't hold their gaze for too long or don't maintain steady eye contact, they may be lying to you. When people speak the truth, they confidently hold the other person's gaze. Remember when your parents or teachers told you to look into their eyes while speaking. However, the knowledge that people who do not look you in the eye has become so common and widely shared that liars and deceivers can now intentionally or purposefully hold their gaze for long.

Manipulation

When a person is holding their gaze continuously without looking away even occasionally, there may be something amiss. The ideal way is to maintain eye contact with a person while looking away at regular intervals.

Increased Nodding

If a person is nodding more than required or nodding in a highly exaggerated way, he or she is worried or concerned about your approval. This can be used to your advantage when it comes to manipulating the person. While addressing a group, always look out for people who are nodding excessively. They are the ones who are worried about your impression of them. These people are subconsciously seeking your approval, which makes them easy manipulation targets.

Stress

How does one detect internal stress through a person's body language? Some of the most common signs of stress are clenched jaws, furrowed brows, fidgeting fingers, and stiff necks. Irrespective of what someone is saying, they may be under some discomfort.

Chapter Four: Reading Body Language and Analyzing People

They may not be very comfortable discussing the topic or thinking about a problem that is clearly causing them anxiety. This is a quick opportunity to seize and play savior if you want to get them to do something.

Catch signs of stress in people to reach out to them and present yourself as a solution to their problems, and eventually persuade or manipulate them into doing what you want! The objective of reading people's body language is to observe a clear difference between their words and body language to understand how they are truly thinking or feeling.

Nervousness

Excessive blinking, fidgeting with their hands, tapping feet, and increased facial movements are all signs of nervousness. Closely observe how people develop jittery feet when they are nervous.

Feet Direction

Watch the direction of a person's feet while communicating with them. The direction of their feet can reveal a lot about what they are thinking at a subconscious level. Since the feet are the most ignored or overlooked part of the body, people do not focus too much on their foot movements or direction. This makes it a powerful subconscious thought-determining mechanism.

If a person's feet are pointed towards the door or exit, they are looking to run away from the place at the first given opportunity. However, if a person's feet are pointed in your direction, they are hooked to the conversation. Whenever you are engaged in an interesting conversation with a person, your foot will involuntarily move forward. It happens at such a subconscious level, which makes it near dependable.

Eye Movements

Our eye movements are closely connected with specific regions of the brain. When you move your eyes in a particular direction, it reveals the brain function that is active. For instance, if you are asked to recall a familiar childhood sound, your eyes will dart slightly up and towards the left to visualize a person or thing that emitted the sound. Then, they move slightly downwards

Chapter Four: Reading Body Language and Analyzing People

followed by movement to the right when you begin recalling the sound or voice.

Our eye movements have a clear pattern (much of NLP or Neuro Linguistic Programming is based on reading people through their eye movements) based on the brain function that is active at a particular time. The brain nerves are closely linked with our eyes to cause very split-second micro eye movements that when you closely observe tell a lot about a person's thought patterns. This is vital information for a manipulator.

When you ask someone something that they can't easily recollect, they eyes will dart to the upper-left direction. This simply indicates that they are attempting to pull out information from past memory. It is widely established that people who are visual learners rely on their visual memory for extracting information. Similarly, if an individual moves their eyes to the upper-left when they are confronted with something, they are not recalling information but rather making it up. In short, they are not telling the truth or answering from memory. Rather, they are trying to make stories.

Manipulation

If they move their eyes to the upper right direction when they are asked something, people are most likely speaking the truth because they are trying to recollect information from their memory before replying. Take for instance: you ask a person where they are returning from, and he/she looks to the upper left instead of upper right, he/she is not recollecting facts but constructing them. This is important information when it comes to manipulating people.

When a person is fighting an internal dilemma, he/she will most likely look towards their left collarbone. This indicates that an individual is thinking deeply about something or engaged in an internal dialogue. For instance, when you confront a person, he or she may be stuck in a dilemma between speaking the truth and lying.

Similarly, when a person darts their eyes quickly from one side to another, it is an indication of telling lies or seeking some form of escape from the situation. They may be afraid of being caught. The person is most likely creating conspiracies in his/her mind.

Chapter Four: Reading Body Language and Analyzing People

When people remember a specific physical sensation experience, their eyes move towards the lower right side. Try to imagine the physical sensation of satin on your skin while keeping your eyes shut. The eyes will reflexively move towards the lower right side.

Attraction

If a person is deeply attracted to you or fixated on a conversation with you, the size of their pupil will invariably expand. Their pupil's contract when the subject of the conversation is boring or the conversation doesn't excite them.

Also, people who are attracted to you may lean in your direction or have their feet pointed towards you. Blinking more than the average blinking rate is also seen as a sign of attraction. If a person blinks over 8-10 times a minute, there's a high chance they are attracted to you. These movements occur at a subconscious level while they are trying to internally process feelings of attraction, which is exactly why blinking is connected with flirting in popular culture.

When someone is charmed by you, their eyes will shine. There is an innately psychological reason behind this. When a person is attracted to someone, their eyes turn a little moist. This reflects more light. Thus, shining eyes along with other above-mentioned clues are an indication of attraction.

Avoiding Errors While Reading Body Language Correctly

Being a master manipulator is about reading people's body language accurately while avoiding potential errors. When you read people correctly, you can tailor your responses according to their thoughts, feelings, and emotions to persuade them into doing exactly what you want. Here are some tips for spotting potential fallacies while reading body language.

Establish a Baseline For Reading People

It is important for establishing a baseline for people's behavior to read them accurately. If you are meeting someone for the first time, you may not really have the opportunity to establish a baseline. However, as far as possible, knowing more about an individual's personality or behavior allows you to gain more reliable information about them through their body

Chapter Four: Reading Body Language and Analyzing People

language. You'll get a more in-depth, accurate, and comprehensive overview of their personality.

For example, let us say a person is hyperactive, quick thinking, and always raring to go. He/she is always up to something and just can't sit still. Their head is full of ideas. Now, if you as a manipulator or people-analyzer do not know this intrinsic fact about the individual's personality, you will most likely misread their body language as nervousness. Tapping their hands and feet, fidgeting with objects, frequently bouncing their legs and more will be viewed as signs of nervousness, when in fact they may be plain restless or wanting to get things done quickly.

If you haven't established a baseline for this person's fundamental personality characteristics, you may end up misreading him or her to conclude that he or she is extremely nervous and not quick-thinking, hyper-energetic and enthusiastic.

You need some background information about a person before determining their thoughts, feelings, and emotions through body language. How does the person generally behave or react in various situations, circumstances, or settings?

Manipulation

How do they generally articulate their thoughts and feelings?

What is their normal voice tone while going through various emotions? Is it different when they are delighted, sad, happy, and excited? How do they reveal their interest or lack of interest in something? All this information will help you read the person in specific settings even more effectively and comprehensively, thus reducing errors when it comes to analyzing people. When a behavior pattern is not consistent with their baseline personality, you can smell something amiss.

Setting or Context

Avoid jumping to a conclusion without taking into consideration the setting or context while reading a person. For example, an individual may be extremely rigid and business-like in the workplace, and casual, gregarious, and leisurely when they meet you outside. The context or setting plays a vital role in determining the behavior of a person. If you read the person outside, you may mistakenly believe them to be someone who is more relaxed and casual about everything, which may not really be the case. It is

Chapter Four: Reading Body Language and Analyzing People

simply the setting that encourages him or her to relax.

The context also plays an important part when it comes to analyzing a person. People may simply cross their arms while sitting because they may be feeling cold and not because they are disinterested or mistrustful of what you are saying. In such a scenario, make the environment more comfortable, or the act of folding their arms and legs will also lead to them switching off from what you are saying on a subconscious level.

Sometimes, people may lean in the opposite direction not because they are trying to escape or are disinterested in the conversation but simply because their seating is uncomfortable. Rubbing their nose may not always be a sign of lying—it can be just cold too. This is why you should look for a bunch of clues (more on it in the next point) to arrive at a near accurate conclusion.

Similarly, look at a variety of non-verbal signals to read the person correctly. Consider everything from a person's body language to their voice to the intonation to understand what they are feeling or thinking. The reading becomes even more power-packed if you add verbal communication or a person's choice of words and phrases to the reading.

The setting is extremely important while reading a person. For example, a person is being interviewed for a position. They may be nervous as people generally are during a job interview. In such a situation, they may not maintain eye contact or move their hand over their face several times (out of nervousness). This doesn't necessarily mean he or she is not speaking the truth or resorting to deception. It simply means they are nervous in the high-pressure setting of a job interview.

Look for a Bunch of Clues

One of the biggest blunders people make while reading or analyzing people is to single out clues rather than study them as a cluster. Avoid looking for isolated, standalone clues and look for a group of clues. For instance, if you read about establishing eye contact as a sign of honesty, trust, and authenticity solely by the fact that an individual is not maintaining consistent eye contact, you may quickly to jump to the conclusion that he or she is a liar.

Chapter Four: Reading Body Language and Analyzing People

On the other side, only by the fact that a person maintains consistent eye contact throughout the conversation, you may falsely deduce that he or she is a confident person who is speaking the truth.

You may ignore all other non-verbal signals such as increased perspiration, twitching toes and hands touching the face frequently to falsely conclude that the person is, in fact, telling the truth simply because he or she is maintaining eye contact. To arrive at an accurate reading about a person's thought patterns, feelings, or emotions; you need to consider a cluster of clues including their expressions, posture, walk, voice, features, and more.

It may be easy to mislead people with a single clue, but it is near impossible to fake all the signals together. The process happens at a very subconscious level, and it is not possible to focus on faking every aspect of our non-verbal behavior to throw others off guard. Therefore, when you are reading a person with the intention of manipulating them to get what you want them to do, look for a cluster of clues that help you read them more reliably.

Manipulation

Cultural Context

Some expressions and gestures such as smiling, eye contact and several other non-verbal signals are universal. They mean the same and are understood across multiple cultures as having similar connotations. However, there are certain gestures, movements, and expressions that have different interpretations across cultures. You this may lead to you misreading another person's thought patterns or emotions based on the non-verbal signals within your culture. Have a clear cultural baseline for reading people's behavior, so you don't end up analyzing it through the filter of your culture.

For example, people in the Italian culture are believed to be loud, gregarious and vivacious in the manner through which they express themselves. Their gestures are animated and enthusiastic. They also speak in an excited, high pitched tone, marked by exuberant screaming and shouting. This is the manner through which they communicate their excitement, delight, and affection.

Someone who comes from Great Britain or another more restrained culture where

Chapter Four: Reading Body Language and Analyzing People

excitement or enthusiasm is more underplayed may not be able to interpret these non-verbal signs accurately. When you view a person's verbal and non-verbal communication patterns in a cultural frame, it becomes simpler to read them correctly.

Even similar gestures can have different interpretations across cultures. For example, a thumbs-up gesture can represent validation or best wishes in western countries. However, the same thumbs-up sign is not considered a culturally appropriate gesture in some Middle Eastern regions. It is seen as rude and inappropriate.

Chapter Five:
Secret Social and Subconscious Manipulation Strategies

While manipulators are generally consciously and purposefully aggressive while fulfilling their agenda, the most dangerous form of manipulation is subconscious manipulation. It occurs at a deeper level and preys on the victim's psychological feelings unlike conscious manipulation where the person dominates, screams, and lies to get what they want.

Why does subconscious manipulation go undetected?

The techniques are subtle and not explicit.

Victims of subconscious manipulation may have a gut reaction or even unpleasant feeling about the manipulator. However, since it isn't explicit or they aren't able to consciously recognize it, they can't logically explain the dynamics of what they are experiencing.

The tactics are often disguised in a more positive garb.

A master subconscious manipulator or persuader may alter their behavior into demonstrating that they are caring, kind, concerned, or crusading to hide their negative agenda. For instance, if the victim reacts negatively to your insults or subtle subconscious attacks, you label them hypersensitive or overly emotional, which they fight challenging to defend.

It is precisely for this reason that manipulation victims are led to feel weak, insecure and uncertain about their beliefs. This leaves them weak and open, which only allows you, as a manipulator, to penetrate deeper into their subconscious.

Exploiting weaknesses

Manipulators will continuously exploit a person's weaknesses and insecurities to exploit them to fulfill their agenda. They will rationalize it as something that the victim deserves. The victims

Chapter Five: Secret Social and Subconscious Manipulation Strategies

generally become blind to their weaknesses or insecurities and completely deny that someone is taking advantage of them. People generally lack the self-knowledge to detect or face their own subconscious vulnerabilities, which you as a manipulator can cash in on. For instance, a buyer who has fallen for a sales tactic will tend to rationalize or justify their purchase over-analyzing their own deep-seated subconscious vulnerability.

Here's looking at some secret and covert manipulation techniques that are widely used by master manipulators to persuade people into doing what they (the manipulators wants).

Create Problems and Offer Solutions

This is a favorite social and subconscious manipulation technique used by master manipulators across the world. As a manipulator, you create an imaginary problem or issue for creating or stimulating a particular reaction from the victim or public at large. The manipulator then sneakily introduces a solution to the problem he or she himself or herself has created.

Manipulation

For instance, first political outfits may allow city violence or fringe terrorist groups to thrive by cleverly overlooking their activities. This will be quickly followed by bringing about an awareness of how people's security is the administration or political outfit's primary concern. They will focus on how they will go all out for strengthening security measures for ensuring public safety.

Manipulators cleverly create a problem and then present a solution for their problems without letting anyone realize that they are responsible for constructing the problems in the first place to come across as heroes for solving people's problems. You become a solution provider this way, which makes it easier for you to get people to act in a certain manner.

The Bitter Pill or Painful Reality

Consider this example carefully to understand how it works as a subconscious level. Your manager urges everyone within the organization to do overtime or pitch in addition work hours. You'll not have to stay up late post work and sometimes even come to the office during weekends. Bitter? Yes of course!

Chapter Five: Secret Social and Subconscious Manipulation Strategies

However, this will be quickly followed up by leading the workforce to believe that there is a high chance of people being laid off within the organization. If people want to keep their jobs, they will have to step up and cover that extra mile for surviving. As a manipulator, your boss may drown you with facts and statistics about how companies who haven't worked on large projects were unable to sustain their operation and other costs and ultimately closed down.

Manipulators often present a situation where they want to get people to do what they want as a bitter pill that has to be taken for the overall good. In the above example, the managers will persuade you about how your sacrifices can have a huge impact in safeguarding the company's future. This again works on a very subconscious level to project something that causes discomfort as a necessary evil. The manipulator will go on about how they don't really want to do something, but there is just no other way out.

Be a Skilled Debater and Public Speaker

Skilled debaters and public speakers find it easy to influence people on a subconscious level through their words. They can prey on people's subconscious feelings and influence them into taking the required action.

Sign up for a public speaking class if you want to be a master manipulator or develop people-convincing skills. You will develop the ability to communicate your ideas in a compelling, assertive, authoritative, arresting, and impressive manner.

Have you ever noticed how some of history's best speakers were able to hypnotize people through their speeches accompanied by the right non-verbal signals? People utilize everything from the tone of their voice to their gestures to the right actions and words to influence people in a specific direction of thought.

Observe how influencers and powerful leaders use their voice and tone to leave behind the right impression.

Conclusion

Thank you again for buying this book!

I hope this book was able to help you understand the basic and advanced manipulation techniques and how they can be used in your daily life to get exactly what you want.

The next step is to simply use all the tried and tested strategies, tips, and techniques mentioned in this valuable resource to control people's minds and influence them into doing what you want them to without them even realizing it.

The book is packed with practical tips, real-life examples and proven strategies to help you get a good grip of the art of manipulation, and how to use it resourcefully to get people to feel, think, and behave in a manner you want them to.

Finally, if you enjoyed this book, then I'd like to ask you for a favor, would you be kind enough to leave a review for this book on Amazon? It'd be greatly appreciated!

Manipulation

Thank you and good luck!

Hypnosis

----- ❧❧❧❧ -----

How to Hypnotize, Influence, and Control Anyone

David T Abbots

Table of Contents

Introduction 193

Chapter 1: Hypnosis 101 195

Chapter 2: Hypnosis Techniques 217

Chapter 3: Best Practices 253

Conclusion 267

Introduction

Congratulations on purchasing this book and thank you for doing so.

By the time you finish reading this book, you will learn how to hypnotize anyone, including yourself. The following chapters will teach you everything that you need to know about hypnosis:

Chapter 1 discusses the basics of hypnosis. Learning the fundamentals is important as it will give you a strong foundation and understanding of what hypnosis is really all about.

Chapter 2 talks about the powerful and effective techniques that you can use to hypnotize anyone and put them under your control or influence.

Chapter 3 lays down the best practices that you should observe to increase your chances of success. Be sure to apply these practices to become an expert at hypnosis.

This is not a book that will just discuss what hypnosis is. Rather, this book will teach you the

Hypnosis

specific steps and techniques on how you can effectively hypnotize people.

There are plenty of books on this subject on the market, thanks again for choosing this one! Every effort was made to ensure it is full of as much useful information as possible. Please enjoy!

Chapter 1: Hypnosis 101

What is Hypnosis?

The term, hypnosis, is commonly defined as a "state of human consciousness involving focused attention and reduced peripheral awareness and an enhanced capacity to respond to suggestion." Many people consider it to be an art form and a skill. There are two schools of thought on what hypnosis is: the *altered state* and the *nonstate theories*. According to the altered state theories, hypnosis is about altering one's consciousness by placing the subject in a trance state, which heightens his state of awareness. However, the nonstate theories claim that hypnosis is nothing more than an imaginative role enactment.

When a person is hypnotized, it is said that he experiences a heightened level of concentration. During such state, all distractions not related to the purpose are completely blocked out. People who are subjects of hypnosis are also more open to suggestions. However, it should be noted that people do not get hypnotized out of nowhere. Hypnosis involves a procedure that is called *hypnotic induction*. This process is composed of instructions and/or suggestions that will lead the subject to a state of mind that is suitable for hypnosis.

Today, hypnosis is also used for therapeutic purposes. When used for this purpose, it is referred to as *hypnotherapy*. Stage magicians who practice mentalism also make use of hypnosis and refer to it as *stage hypnosis*.

Brief History of Hypnosis

It can be said that hypnotism is as old as man himself. People go in and out of hypnotic states without being aware of it. Hypnotism is also used in various spiritual practices and religions, although they normally do not use the term *hypnosis*. However, in scientific circles, hypnosis only became popular in the 18th century, and it was because of a German doctor named, Franz Mesmer. In fact, he is now known as the Father of Modern Hypnotism. At the time, hypnosis was known as Mesmerism, as taken from the last name of Franz Mesmer. Also, in the medical field, other important figures were John

Chapter 1: Hypnosis 101

Elliotson and James Esdaille. A researcher named, James Braid, also helped to further explore the health benefits of hypnosis.

Hypnosis has been around for thousands of years. The problem is that it mainly concerns the mind, and the human mind is that part of the body that science hasn't been able to understand completely yet.

Hypnosis has been applied in various fields, including entertainment, self-improvement, and also in the military. Although to this date, the American Medical Association does not take any official stand as to the medical uses of hypnosis, the American Medical Association has documented that hypnosis helps increase the efficacy of healing in a clinical setting.

To date, hypnosis is still covered in mystery, and many people are willing to learn and discover its immense potentials.

Does It Work?

Okay, so hypnosis sounds really nice and cool. But, does it work? This is the question that many people are eager to know. The reason why there are different views and opinions on this matter is

Hypnosis

because of what is known as hypnotic susceptibility. This refers to the level or rate by which a person is open to being hypnotized. Yes, some people are easier to hypnotize than others. Just because you use a particular technique on one person does not always mean that you can use the same technique on another and expect for the same effect all the time.

Okay, do not be discouraged. The important point is that hypnosis actually works. When you deal with people that are less susceptible to being hypnotized, then it will only be a bit more challenging, perhaps you will have to use a different technique or be able to execute a technique more effectively. Still, the fact cannot be denied that hypnosis can work on anyone. This is why it is important for you to actually practice the techniques. Learning how to hypnotize people is just like learning a new skill. It is not something that you can just read from books. Rather, you also have to put your knowledge into actual practice to make it work.

Here are some notable experiments and applications of hypnosis:

Chapter 1: Hypnosis 101

Hypnosis has been proven to significantly lower the pain experienced during surgery. Not only that, it also makes the subject less anxious. What is more, even the surgical time is reduced, and it also prevents any complications arising from the procedure.

In the area of cancer, a disease that is very much popular this day and age, hypnosis can also be of help. In several experiments, it was proven that the use of hypnosis significantly alleviated the symptoms of chemotherapy, such as issues with nausea and vomiting.

With respect to the topic of immunity, as reported in the *American Journal of Clinical Hypnosis*, hypnosis is able to raise the activity of cells like B-cells and T-cells, which are key to a more powerful immune response.

In a study that was presented by American Psychological Association Meeting, it shows that the use of hypnosis can also be used in treating children with ADHD.

The American Lung Association also conducted its own study. Among 3,000 smokers, 22% were able to completely quit from smoking just after about a month of being engaged in hypnotic sessions.

Back in 2000, the International Journal of Clinical Experimental Hypnosis published a finding that in 169 test subjects, hypnosis was proven to be significantly successful with alleviating pain and chronic tension headaches.

These are just some of the notable applications of hypnosis. There are still many other studies and experiment that have been done and will still be done. Indeed, the study of hypnosis can create amazing developments and changes in the world.

Busting the Myths

The practice of hypnosis has been around for centuries. Just like other interesting and amazing practices, it is also surrounded by many myths. In order to have the right understanding of what hypnosis is all about, you should learn the truths behind the myths. Let us discuss them one by one:

- Only a few chosen people can learn how to hypnotize

Chapter 1: Hypnosis 101

There are people who think of hypnosis as some sort of a special gift that only a few chosen people possess. However, it should be made clear that everyone can learn how to hypnotize. Yes, *you* can learn how to hypnotize people, including yourself. The problem is that only a few people care to read anything about hypnosis, and even fewer are those who actually take the time and effort to practice it.

Now, there are also people who take some time to learn hypnosis but then end up concluding that it does not work. Why does this happen? Well, there are two main reasons why this happens. The first reason is that they do not acquire the right materials that can teach them how to actually hypnotize people. Instead, they end up with fluff materials that teach nothing substantial about hypnosis. The second reason is that they fail to practice the techniques correctly and regularly. Once again, if you want to learn hypnosis, then make it a priority to actually practice the techniques. Merely reading about hypnosis will not turn you into a hypnotist.

Hypnosis

- Hypnotism is a demonic practice

There are also people who think of the practice of hypnosis to be a demonic practice. They usually associate hypnosis with the occult. Although it is true that occult practices also make use of hypnosis, it does not mean that it is already a demonic practice. For example, prayers are also used in the occult, but it does not mean that praying is considered a demonic practice. Different people use hypnosis for different reasons. It all depends on your intentions and how you use it.

- Some people cannot be hypnotized

It is true that people have different hypnotic susceptibility levels. However, this does not mean that people cannot be hypnotized. In fact, it is safe to say that everyone has already been hypnotized in life one way or another. Take, for example, what happens when a person watches a movie. If this person watches a comedy show, he ends up laughing and being happy. However, if he watches a drama show, chances are that he would feel sad and gloomy. In the same way, if he watches a horror film, then he would feel afraid. This is also a form of hypnotism whereby

Chapter 1: Hypnosis 101

a person feels and acts in a certain way. Another experiment that you can do is to talk with someone about something he is not interested in. Soon enough, you will make him feel bored. Another good example would be observing how businesses promote or market their products on the TV. Do you notice how so many people suddenly want to buy a product just because they have seen a commercial on the TV? Again, hypnotism takes its role. Of course, these are just simple experiments of how hypnotism is used to a certain extent even by laymen. If you find it hard to hypnotize someone, chances are that you should change the technique that you use to hypnotize him, or you simply probably need more practice.

- Hypnotism is hard to do

Just because most people do not know how to use hypnotism effectively does not mean that it is hard to do. The problem is that most people do not even take the time and efforts to study hypnotism. Also, it should be noted that hypnotism is also a skill. It is not enough that you just rely on gaining mental intellect. Even if you read all the books and articles about hypnotism, it would not be enough to actually allow you to hypnotize and influence anyone effectively. Again, there are two important parts of learning hypnosis: You need to gain the right knowledge, and then you have to put that knowledge into actual and regular practice.

Just like learning any other skill, the level of difficulty of the different techniques may vary. In the next chapter, you as you learn the different hypnotic techniques, you might notice that some techniques seem easier for you to do than others. Feel free to explore the techniques and identify the ones that seem most suitable to you. It does not really matter what technique you use; the important thing is that it works.

6 Little-Known Truths About Hypnosis

I.   You do not need a hypnotist

Normally, people perceive hypnosis to be composed of two parties: the one who is doing the hypnotism and the one being hypnotized. Although this is true, it is not always the case. There is also what is called self-hypnotism. It usually makes use of autosuggestions to allow you to influence your subconscious mind. In effect, this will allow you to make changes to your mood and behavior. Many experts suggest

Chapter 1: Hypnosis 101

that you learn self-hypnosis as it is one of the best ways to study and learn the hypnosis.

II. The American Medical Association approved hypnotism for medical and psychology applications

Yes, the American Medical Association was fully convinced of the effectiveness of hypnotism that, they approved it for both medical and psychology use. This approval happened back in the 1950s. However, around 20 years later, they withdrew their approval. Still, many hypnotists continue to use this practice. Even today, there are many practitioners who make use of hypnosis techniques in treating their subjects. Not to mention, study and research on the subject are still being made. Since hypnotism is very much associated with the mind, it can be said that there is too much to learn about it as it explores the vast potentials and capabilities of the human mind.

III. The term *hypnosis* means sleep

The word, hypnosis, means sleep. However, it should be noted that you do not actually fall asleep when you are hypnotized. Come to think of it, if the subject were asleep, then he would not be able to do anything. Rather, the subject is placed in a different state of consciousness which may look like being asleep, but the subject is actually conscious throughout.

IV. The army relied on hypnosis to make amputations and other treatments

During the Civil War, the army surgeons relied on using hypnotic techniques to perform major and minor operations on the injuries suffered by the soldiers. At that time, there was nothing strange about it. The use of hypnosis was considered normal and part of the regular medical procedure.

V. Hypnosis is an effective pain fighter

So many experiments have already been conducted to prove just how hypnosis can be used to effectively combat pain, whether during an operation or otherwise. These experiments, which were mostly conducted by professionals and doctors, were mostly successful. Indeed, it is already a fact that hypnosis can remove or at least decrease the level of pain to a significant degree.

Chapter 1: Hypnosis 101

VI. Hypnosis can have different results

Again, this is due to people having varying level of hypnotic susceptibility, also known as *hypnotizability*. This is also why a certain technique may work on one person greatly but fail to create any noticeable effect on another. Some people may feel really good after undergoing a certain hypnotic session, while others might not feel that well about it. This is also why hypnosis has to be conducted by a trained professional who truly understands what he is doing.

The 3 Phases of a Hypnosis Act

Hypnotism is a process. It does not happen in an instant. There are essentially three main stages to any hypnotic act. Let us examine them one by one:

➢ Preparation

The first phase is the preparation. This is where you set a goal and create a good rapport with the subject. You should identify the problem, if any, as well as the outcome or change that you want to happen. It is also during this phase where you should asses how susceptible your client is to hypnotism. Consider this phase as the part of where you get to know more about the subject and create a good relationship with him. It is also at this point where you make the subject feel relaxed being with you. Remember that relaxation is important to any hypnotic act. If the subject is not relaxed enough, then it would be hard to give him any suggestions.

This phase does not just refer to you as the hypnotist, but it also involves your subject. If doing self-hypnosis, then obviously this is about yourself. However, when working on people, then be sure to include your subject. This means creating a good rapport with your subject. If the subject is not comfortable with you, then it would be more difficult to hypnotize him. So, an important part of this stage is to make the subject feel at ease with you. Of course, you should also feel comfortable with your subject. Engaging in small talks is a good way to do this. In fact, many hypnotic techniques are applied during such "off" moments when the subject is not aware that he will be the subject of a hypnotic act. It is also worth noting that the more that you know about the subject, the easier it will be to hypnotize him, as you can more

Chapter 1: Hypnosis 101

easily identify the best technique to use and how you should employ it.

Preparation does not need to take a long time. You do not need to know too much about your subject. It is enough to just have an idea of how you two get along together. All it takes is to simply spend time with the person and see how it goes. Although establishing a good relationship is ideal, you do not actually need to create a very strong bond. It is enough to simply establish good rapport with your subject. But, of course, the more that your subject trusts you, the better it will be.

> **Induction**

This is the part where you apply the techniques to hypnotize the client. You can use your authority, certain hypnotic words, imagery, music, and even the environment. Another part of induction is known as Deepening. This is simply taking it a step further and actually fully hypnotizing your subject to make him actually act the way you would want him to. Others would also recommend adding what is known as *utilization* or putting into words the outcome that you desire. However, this is a matter of

Hypnosis

personal preference as it can sometimes make things too obvious, especially if you intend to hypnotize the subject secretly. Although this phase is the most important phase, it should be noted that the first and last phases are also important as there is nothing in the process that you can just ignore.

Since you do not intend to use hypnotism as a type of hypnotherapy, as you wouldn't be treating patients but instead trying to control and influence people, you should be very discreet in applying the techniques in this book. You have to apply the techniques smoothly and naturally. You would not want to give the subject any hint or idea that you intend to control him; otherwise, his defenses will be up, and it would be impossible to hypnotize him.

Okay, a common problem is that for hypnotism to be effective, then the subject has to consent. This is the challenge. How can you make the subject give his consent if he/she is not even aware that you intend to hypnotize him? Well, the key here is that the consent does not have to be made expressly. Rather, it is just a matter of having your subject want to follow you and whatever it is that you tell him. It is about making him more open to you so that you can finally enter his mind and control him.

Do not apply a technique that you have not yet practiced. A common mistake is to use a technique without adequate training. Of course, during training, you should use the techniques. Be sure to make it clear when you intend to just practice a technique and when you really need to apply it. When you face important situations, only rely on using the techniques that you have already practiced. Not to mention, it would be very awkward to get caught by the subject that you are trying to control them.

➤ **Termination**

This is where you end the hypnosis and allow the subject to return back to his normal consciousness. If you are doing self-hypnosis, this is usually done by counting backwards or putting all your focus on your physical body.

Termination has to be made just as smoothly as you make the subject enter the induction phase. It is also noteworthy that there are techniques that can give you a headache if you get out of the hypnotic state quickly. Again, when using hypnotic techniques, do not forget that smoothness and the naturalness of the actions are important. It is also a good way to cover the fact that you are hypnotizing a person.

This is the easiest phase. All you need to do is to gently snap the subject out of the hypnotic state. If you use a technique that does not require taking the subject into a deep level, then you can usually terminate the process easily just by asking your subject a question that will make him think. Indeed, making the subject think and use his analytical mind is a good and quick way to get anyone out of the state of hypnotic induction.

How to Use Hypnosis to Influence and Control Other People

Consent is important in any hypnosis act. A common mistake is to think that hypnosis can be used forcefully. This is wrong. You should know that trust is an important part of hypnosis. Hence, when it comes to hypnotizing other people, you should create a good relationship. Of course, you would not want to tell people that you will hypnotize them; otherwise, they would be on their guard, and you would not be able to control or influence them. Instead, you should

Chapter 1: Hypnosis 101

apply the techniques discreetly. Now, it takes practice to control others using hypnosis. The good news is that it is possible, and that you can do it. You simply have to stick to the lessons and techniques in this book.

Of course, before you hypnotize anyone, you should first have an objective in mind. What is it that you want him/her to think, feel, or do? Be clear about this matter. The next thing is to engage and know more about the subject. This will let you identify the best technique to use, as well as how you should apply it for the best result. It is in applying the technique that is the most crucial part. You do not want the subject to know that you want to influence or control him. The key to do this is to have your own realization. Unfortunately, many aspiring hypnotists still fail to realize that they should not force their way into another person's mind or will. Everything should be done smoothly and naturally. There should be no awkward force or pressure of any kind. Instead of using forced commands, give suggestions. In fact, hypnosis is all about giving suggestions that the other person would think and feel most practical and convenient for him. Using force or making the subject feel uneasy is a fast way to snap him out of hypnotic state and could ruin your plan, so be very careful about this.

Also, when it comes to controlling other people, it is also strongly suggested for you to just use self-hypnosis. It is a safe and unobtrusive way to influence the people around you.

It should be noted that this book was not written to influence and control people in a bad way. Remember that as a hypnotist, you are responsible for your actions. Hence, be sure to use your knowledge of hypnotism only in good way and not to unfairly control others.

Self-Hypnosis

Are you having a hard time hypnotizing other people? Well, why not hypnotize the one that is most open to being hypnotized? That person is none other than yourself. In fact, once you learn to hypnotize yourself effectively, then you may realize that there is no need for you to learn how to hypnotize other people. Most of the time, just by making adjustments or changes to yourself, you can already significantly improve how you deal with other people.

Chapter 1: Hypnosis 101

In the next chapter, you will learn hypnotic techniques that you can use on other people, as well as those that you can use on yourself. The best thing about self-hypnosis is that you do not meddle or interfere with other people. Instead, you only deal with yourself. Hence, there is no moral or any ethical issue for you to worry about. Also, hypnotizing one's self is usually easier since you would not have to deal with any trust issues. In fact, if you are just starting out to learn hypnosis, many experts suggest that you begin by doing self-hypnosis.

When practicing self-hypnosis, remember to focus on employing the techniques instead of thinking that you are only fooling yourself. An important part of hypnosis is to change the subject's state of mind. When you apply self-hypnosis, stop asking yourself if you are doing it right. Instead, just apply the technique properly. It is a matter of doing and not thinking.

Needless to say, self-hypnosis also takes practice. When you hypnotize yourself, then you should try to just relax and be very open. Some people find this hard to do. For some reason, end up being defensive even to themselves. If ever this becomes an issue, just remember to keep on practicing. You will soon get used to it. The key is to expose yourself to the techniques in this book until they become second nature to you. Last but not least, remember to always engage in actual practice.

Chapter 2: Hypnosis Techniques

Now that you have a better understanding of what hypnosis is about, it is time for you to learn the different techniques that you can use to hypnotize anyone, including yourself:

Hypnotic Breathing

This technique is to be used for self-hypnosis, and it uses the power or rhythm of the breath. We continue to breathe and yet seldom pay any attention to it. If the rhythm stops for a few minutes, that would mean death. This is how important breathing is; it is life. This technique is about placing your focus on the single and most important act that you ever do: breathing. This technique will bring you into a light trance or a heightened state of consciousness which makes you open to suggestions. If you are interested in self-hypnosis (and you should be), then this is a basic technique that you ought to master. The steps are as follows:

Hypnosis

Close your eyes and relax. Focus on your breathing. Breathe in gently and breathe out. Put all your focus on your breath. If other thoughts appear in your mind, gently ignore them and put your focus back on your breath. Breathe in and out gently. Soon enough, you will be in a different state of mind, like a light trance. Just continue this simple meditation exercise. When you are ready to get back to ordinary consciousness, simply think of your body and count from 10 to 1. Slowly move your fingers and toes and open your eyes.

Feel free to do this exercise with your eyes open. The important thing is to be as relaxed as possible and to focus on your breathing. This is a basic meditation exercise that is often used in self-hypnosis as it offers an easy and effective way to be in a trance where suggestions can easily be made. Of course, this of itself will not hypnotize you in any way. However, this forms the foundation of many self-hypnotic techniques, so this is definitely worth learning. From this state of mind, you can use affirmation and many other self-hypnotic statements to create a change in yourself.

Chapter 2: Hypnosis Techniques

It should also be noted that as you do this exercise, it is strongly suggested to keep your spine straight. You might want to do it in a sitting position since lying down can lead you to fall asleep.

It is amazing how the brain and the body follow the breath. Did you know that if you breathe slowly and gently, then you will soon feel relaxed? It can be said that one's state of mind follows the state of his breathing. Therefore, by controlling your breath, you are also able to control your mind. Here lies the enormous secret of the mind that is still considered a mystery.

Affirmations

Affirmations are also known as autosuggestions. They are composed of statements that you repeat over and over again allowing their meaning to sink into the subconscious, which can soon create a change. Now, there are certain points that you need to take note of when you use this technique. First, it is important to be able to frame your statement of affirmation correctly. Of course, before you do this, you first need to know what you want to happen or change. This way you will know the kind of affirmation that you need to make. Once you figure this out, then you can start creating your statement of affirmation. You should keep your statement short, direct, and clear. It is also advised that you keep it positive; hence, avoid using the word "not." For example, instead of saying, "I am not feeling bad." you should say, "I am feeling better." You should also keep it in the present tense instead of in the future tense. Therefore, do not say, "I will be able to control myself." Instead, say, "I am able to control myself." Although these are just simple guidelines, they are nonetheless very important and effective.

So, how do you use autosuggestion? Well, you are probably familiar with how you would cheer yourself up when you are feeling down. You would say, "It is going to be okay." Autosuggestion works the same way. However, you will do it in a more effective manner. It is important that you craft your statement of affirmation carefully since it is the foundation of this technique. Once you have your statement, you simply have to repeat it over and over again. Now, some people just repeat it without even giving it any attention. This can also work. However, it is also good, if not better, if you focus on it as you say the words. It is also very

Chapter 2: Hypnosis Techniques

important to believe whatever it is that you are saying. This is some kind of a trick of the mind, call it sleight of mind, if you would, but this technique really works if you practice it regularly. The way to say your statement is either out loud or in your mind. You should repeat it in a comfortable pace like a chant.

When should you recite your statement of affirmation? Well, you can do it at any time. Although it is advised that you do it while engaged in a hypnotic breathing meditation, you can still use autosuggestion at any time, even right now or while driving — any time. The idea is to repeat it so that it sinks into your subconscious. You then simply have to wait and trust your subconscious to make the necessary changes over time.

Do not feel discouraged if nothing happens in the first few times that you do this. Just keep on practicing. The more that you practice this technique the better you will get.

It is also important to note that you should only use a single statement at a time. Using more than one statement can confuse your mind. So, take as much time as you can. Focus on one thing that you want to change in yourself and do not allow your energy to be divided. Do not worry; once the change materializes, then you can shift to another goal.

Although the use of affirmations is very simple, it is also very effective. This is why when you read books on self-hypnosis, you will often read about the use of autosuggestion.

If you use this for self-hypnosis, it is suggested that you use your autosuggestions just before going to sleep. In a study, it was found that the closer you are to sleep, the more that you make use of your subconscious mind. During such time, it becomes much easier to influence the subconscious mind. Feel free to recite your statement of affirmation out loud or even silently in your mind until you fall asleep.

The use of affirmations is one of the basic techniques in self-hypnosis. It is considered as basic not because it is very simple but because it is very important and effective. It would be strange for you not to know about it if you want to be a successful hypnotist.

You can also use affirmations on other people. This time, you refer to them as *suggestions*. It works the same way except that you refer to the other person. For example, instead of saying, "I am getting stronger." You can tell the other person, "You are getting stronger." If the subject does not know how to use autosuggestion, then be the one to do it for him.

Hypnotic Bind Technique

This is one of the most popular techniques used in hypnosis. There is really nothing extraordinary about this technique. In fact, parents usually apply it when they deal with their kids. This is where you give someone a choice usually by using an either/or question. Here is an example: Would you like to study or brush your teeth? Either way, you get to make someone do what you want. It is not about asking if a person would like to do something, but it is about just asking which one he would like to do. Regardless of which option he chooses, you will surely win since you get to make him do something.

There is also what is known as double blind technique. When you use this technique, you appear to make him choose between two options but which all lead to the same result. Here is an example: Would you like to take a bath in five or ten minutes? Either way, you get to make him do the action that you want. Of course, this technique does not just work on children. You can use the same technique on adults. For example: Would you like to have lunch in 10 or 15 minutes?

This technique presumes that the subject would want to do something. In doing so, the subject is left with no choice but just to give an answer. Just be careful with this technique as some people can notice how it works. Do it smoothly and naturally to avoid raising any doubts.

You should execute this technique smoothly. If you hesitate, then chances are that the subject will notice it and have his defenses up. When this happens, then this technique might be compromised.

Handshake Technique

The use of this technique was made popular by Milton Erickson, who is also known as the father of hypnotherapy. It is a good way to quickly induce hypnotic trance as it catches the subject when he is off guard. Normally, a handshake is used as a form of greeting in a social situation.

Chapter 2: Hypnosis Techniques

This technique takes advantage of this and uses it as a way to disrupt the common norm by interrupting the usual mind pattern. The way to do this is either by grabbing the subject's wrist or pulling him to cause him to be off balanced. Once the usual pattern is interrupted, then the subconscious mind opens up to hypnotic suggestions. This is the best time for you to whisper or say something to your subject to hypnotize him.

This technique takes practice, so do not be discouraged if it does not work in your first few attempts. The problem with this technique is that it is hard to practice it, especially when you are just starting out. Since it often causes your subject to be out of balance, it would be quite difficult to come up an excuse for your actions. Tip: just relax and act naturally.

Eye Cue

The brain is divided into two: The left side is the practical and subconscious side, while the right portion of the brain is the one responsible for creativity, and it is also the conscious side. By looking at the subject's eyes, you will be able to see which part of the brain he/she is currently more active on. If the subject is looking to is right, then he is probably trying to access the conscious part of their brain, or is he looking to the left which means that he is on his subconscious and is open to suggestions? By being observant and using proper timing, you are able to influence the subject and feed him with suggestions.

Again, this technique takes time and practice to master. You simply have to get used to it. At first, you might find it hard to pay attention to where your subject is looking, but this will soon be easy for you to do.

Another way to use this technique is to tempt the subject to look at the direction where you want him to focus on. For purposes of making suggestions, you would want him to look to his left. A good way to do this is by using gestures. Gesture with your hand and make him look to his left side. You can also sit yourself in such a way that he would be more inclined to lean to his left to talk to you. This way, he will be more susceptible to suggestions.

Do not stare at the eyes of the subject for too long; otherwise, you might make him feel

Chapter 2: Hypnosis Techniques

uncomfortable. Instead, just act naturally as if you were engaged in any normal conversation. Again, this technique requires practice, so do not be surprised if you find it quite uncomfortable to do during the first few times that you try it out.

Visualization

Use visualization to induce trance and feed suggestions to your subject. The process does not have to be too formal or solemn. You can use this technique even when engaged in a casual conversation simply by saying, "Just imagine..." You can then add in the details that you want. During which, you can also add in your suggestions. Another way to do this is to remind your subject of a particular event that he is well familiar with. This way, you would not have to tell him what to visualize. For example, you can ask something like this: Do you remember Kate's birthday party at her house? This way, you already set the scene without telling your subject directly what to think about. While the subject tries to recall the details, his mind becomes more open to suggestions. This is the best time for you to get into his mind and give suggestions.

Hypnosis

The use of visualization is one of the most effective tools of a hypnotist. Once you are able to make people visualize something, you can easily add details to it and put him under your control. Indeed, one of the best ways to enter the mind of a person is by accessing his very thoughts, and there is no better way of doing this than making him use his imagination and leading that imagination to your will. Of course, you should still be discrete about this. Make him feel in control of everything although you are already exercising full dominion over his thoughts.

Visualization is commonly used in self-hypnosis. For example, if you want to relax, just visualize yourself in a relaxing place like the beach. Just spend time in this visualization and you will soon feel the effect. There is a saying in Stoicism, "The quality of your happiness depends upon the quality of your thoughts." The same applies in hypnosis, especially in self-hypnosis. This is why if you want to feel good and fill yourself with positive energy, then you should fill your mind with happy and positive thoughts. Of course, you would want to avoid the opposite as no one would want to be full of negativity. Indeed, the use of visualization is one of the best ways to

Chapter 2: Hypnosis Techniques

influence your own mind. And, here is the secret: Once you can influence your own mind, then you can also influence everything around you. As the saying goes, "If you want to change the world, change yourself."

Foot Trip

This is not a recommended method, yet it is a good technique if only you can practice it. Be sure to use this with caution. When a person is shocked, his mind opens and allows you to feed it with information that you want. The way to apply this technique is by shocking the subject by tripping his foot and allowing him to fall, just be kind enough to catch him before he hits the ground. This was also used by Milton Erickson with positive results. As the subject is falling, his mind becomes very open to suggestions, and that is your best moment to talk to him and give him suggestions. Although it is good to be aware of this technique, it should be noted that this is not a suggested method, and especially stay away from using this technique if you are an absolute beginner.

Body Scan

This is another effective technique for self-hypnosis. As the name implies, it is about scanning your body. This time, you simply have to do it with your mind. The steps are as follows:

Assume a comfortable position, preferably lying down with your spine straight. Now, slowly scan your body with your mind. Bring your attention to your head and feel it. Now, bring your attention to your neck and feel it with your mind. Continue to scan your body this way, part by part. By the time you finish scanning your body, you will be in a trance. You can then use autosuggestion or visualization to give suggestions to your mind.

Once you get used to his technique, you will be able to do it at any time even while walking. However, it is important that you use this technique regularly for you to improve and get used to it.

Indirect Suggestion

This is another favorite technique used by Erickson. Instead of taking an authoritative role, you interact with your subject in a gentle

Chapter 2: Hypnosis Techniques

manner. This is an excellent technique to use if you know that your subject is someone who is skeptical of being in a trance or are not that open to suggestions. The key to using this technique is to learn to reword your statement. For example, instead of just telling your subject to close his eyes, you can use the word "might," such as, "You might want to close your eyes if you are feeling relaxed." You should also remember to pay attention to your tone of voice. You do not want to sound authoritarian. Instead, you should use a gentle approach.

Direct Suggestion

From time to time, you may want to use direct suggestion. Although not a recommended approach, it is nonetheless still effective as long as you use it in the right situation. Take note that you cannot use this technique at all times. Before you use it, you must first ensure that the subject is very much open to suggestions and that he should somehow depend on you for direction. This way, he will have to accept whatever you tell him. A good way to do this is if you notice that your subject is dependent on you and has full trust in you.

Hypnosis

If you have a conversation with someone who sees you as an expert in the topic of your conversation, then you can easily employ this approach. This is because you can more easily exercise your authority. However, do not abuse it too much to the point that he might feel that you are bossing him around. Nobody would want that. Speak with authority and respectfully.

Warm Reading

The more that a person agrees to whatever you say, the more he becomes open to suggestions from you. A good and effective to do this is by using this technique. So, how do you apply it and make people agree? The way to do it is to make statements that are agreeable to everyone, or at least almost everyone. For example, "You feel happy when you are with your friends."

Cold Reading

You are probably familiar with how this works. If you have seen how people use spirit boards, then this is also how it works. You do this by asking a series of simple questions. For example, you can say, "You look sad." If the person responds in the affirmative, you ask another question that is answerable by yes or no. For example, "Is it

Chapter 2: Hypnosis Techniques

because you failed the exam?" Just stick to asking questions answerable by yes or no and allow the person to explain if he/she wants to. This is also a good way to build trust as the person learns to open up to you. Of course, if you do this, then you will have to listen to the person well.

Misdirection

Misdirection is often used, even in the real world. Those in business, entertainment, and politics, are quite good at this. The prefix *mis* means wrong; hence, it means leading someone to a wrong direction. However, if used in hypnotism, it takes a different meaning. In this case, you simply change the direction of the person's mind and direct it to something that is more positive in nature. For example, if the person is feeling stressed out and anxious, say, "As you become anxious, see yourself having a good time at the beach." In everyday dealings, you can easily apply this technique by turning every negative thought into something positive with just a simple shift in focus of the mind. It is all about turning an unpleasant image, thought, or idea, into something good.

Hypnosis

Although referred to as a misdirection, when applied to hypnosis, you actually direct the person to where you want his mind to be. You misdirect him from his usual way of thinking to the state of mind where you want him to be.

It can be said that the whole hypnotic act is an act of misdirection where you continuously lead the person to what you want him to think and/or feel. Of course, the way to do this is to get into his mind and make him think of thoughts to influence him. When you use this technique, you should be careful with the use of your words. Remember that it is through your words that you will get into the mind of your subject and give him suggestions. Once you make him visualize something, you should also visualize the same scenery or image in your mind. This way you are able to picture and follow what your subject is perceiving in his mind. All that you need to do now is to add more details as you add in your own suggestions. Since you also visualize the image in your mind, you are able to gauge the message that you are sending to your subject.

When making use of visualization, encourage your subject to use as many senses as possible. This is the way to increase the effectiveness of

Chapter 2: Hypnosis Techniques

any visual image. Do not just see it, but also involve as many senses as possible. For example, if you make your subject visualize a sea, also mention about the movement of the waves, the feeling of the wind on the skin, the heat of the sun, the sound of birds in the distance, and others. The more senses you involve in the visualization the more it will appear real to your subject, which significantly increases the effectiveness of the technique.

Although you want your subject to engage in visualization, avoid committing the mistake of getting too caught up with the images. Remember that you are only using visualization as a means to hypnotize your subject. So, be sure to also deliver the right message through the images or scenes that you make him think about.

Reframing

This technique is usually applied as some kind of metaphor. This is a good way to create a change in perception in the mind of your subject. Let us assume that your subject tells you that he wants to lose weight. However, instead of living a healthy lifestyle, he spends his day sitting and playing on his computer. You can talk to him about his interest: the game. And then explain to him how much time and efforts he spends to level up his character to excel on the game. You can then compare it with how it is like if you want to lose weight. You also need to give it time and effort. By having a point of comparison, you can more easily reframe the mind of your subject not only to make him understand something better but also to encourage him to take action.

Reframing is a good way to make a person understand something using comparison. If you find that the subject fails to understand something that you want him to analyze, then this is an excellent technique to use to make him understand it better.

Future Pacing

This technique lets a person realize the possible consequences of his actions. You can do this as a form of self-hypnosis or if you want to hypnotize others. So, how does it work? The steps are as follows:

Before you do anything, take some time to think about it. See yourself already doing it. How does it make you feel? For example, before you buy a particular dress, imagine yourself

Chapter 2: Hypnosis Techniques

already in possession of it and wearing it. Are you really happy and satisfied with it? By visualizing the results of your actions, you can avoid making the wrong decisions.

Of course, this technique does not just work for self-hypnosis. You can do the same and apply it on another. For example, if a friend tells you that he feels hesitant to buy a new skateboard, ask him to visualize himself skating using the skateboard he wants to buy, would he be really happy with it? It is good to take as much time as possible with this technique. After all, it is for free and can allow you to prevent wrong decisions. It also lets you realize the consequences of the actions that you intend to do. Of course, this does not just work whenever you want to buy something, but it also applies to everything.

When you use this technique, you need to accept it if you realize that a certain course of action might not be the best action to take. When this happens, then be disciplined enough to change your course of action or simply not to take an action. In the same way, if you find that your subject is still hesitant despite already imagining himself doing what he thinks he wants to do, then you should ask him questions to make him realize if that is really something that he wants.

Many people have made wrong decisions in life simply because they failed to exercise some future pacing. Do not let the same mistakes happen to you. There are so many instances in life to apply future pacing. For example, you can think about the direction of your career, your personal life, and others. It is just up to you to take advantage of it and see what might happen. When you use this technique, remember to take as much time as you need, and also consider all possibilities that may happen along the way.

Naming

There is no word sweeter to the ears than a person's name. If you want to get someone's attention, just say his name. A study also shows that people will tend to buy from someone who has the same or similar name to his. Instead of using the name and if you are just talking to a single person, you can simply say *you*. Still, it should be noted that it is still advised that you use the person's name. You do not have to use the real name of the person. You might want to use his nickname or whatever name he prefers.

Chapter 2: Hypnosis Techniques

The key is to make him hear you say his name. Needless to say, when you use this technique, you should pronounce the name correctly and properly.

By saying the person's name, you do not just get his attention, but you also make him feel good at the same time. This is true, especially if you say his name in a nice and pleasant manner. This is another reason why it is important to take note of the person you are speaking with. For some reason, people also trust more easily those people who call them by their name. It simply creates a better familiarity and closeness. If you want to build trust and rapport with your subject (you should), then it is an excellent idea to start mentioning his name when you call and talk to him.

Because...

If you deal with people whom you think are very logical, then be sure to use the hypnotic word *because*. Why is this hypnotic word? Well, many people are easily convinced if something is backed up with reason or logic. Hence, simply using the word *because* can make whatever you say seem more believable. Of course, you should also come up with a good reason. Still, sometimes you might not even need a good reason. As long as people hear the word *because* they just conclude that it is a good choice. However, this may not apply to all people so to be safe be sure to back it up with good reasons. The more logical and reasonable it appears, the better. It does not have to complicated; you can just use simple reasons if you want. The important thing is to have a good reason and let the other person know about it. This is a technique that you can use if you intend to convince someone or even if you only want to try to convince yourself.

This is also a good technique to use to convince someone to share the same view as you have. You do not always have to exactly use the word *because*. The important thing here is to come up with justifiable reasons to support your view or argument to persuade your target to take your side.

Ask Questions

There is so much that can be realized simply by asking questions. However, do not waste the time of your client with just meaningless

Chapter 2: Hypnosis Techniques

questions. Instead, you have to ask the right questions. The right questions are those that will make him realize something that you want him to realize by himself. You can do this by asking a series of questions and continuously digging into the subject. Let the other person come up with his reasons and own realization. Just stick to the topic and ask questions, especially the question *why*.

Some people find it uncomfortable to ask questions. After all, how can you tell if the subject is even interested in answering them? Well, the way to do this is to ask questions about a topic that you know that your subject likes to talk about, such as his hobbies or anything that he is interested in. If you do this, not only will he answer your questions, but he will also enjoy answering your questions. This is an effective and easy way to establish a good rapport quickly. Continue to ask questions and stick to the topic unless the subject appears to want to talk about something else. The important thing is to keep the conversation flowing and let the subject think and have his own realizations.

As you can see, this technique is about helping your subject go through the thinking process until he ends up with his own conclusion, which is exactly the realization that you want him to learn. However, this is a politer way of telling the subject what to do instead of demanding for something or giving commands. Just be careful; you do not want your subject to end up with a wrong realization, so be sure to guide him properly. For example, if you want to convince someone that he should stop taking illegal drugs, be sure to lead the flow of conversation towards a realization that taking drugs is not a good idea.

Instead of telling someone what to do in the form of a command, make him realize why what you want is the best option. After all, many people do not enjoy being told what they should do. So, simply help him realize it by asking questions.

Mirroring

This is a very effective hypnotic technique. As the term implies, it is where you mirror the other person. So, how does it work? Well, simply pay attention to the body position of your subject. Now, you simply have to copy it. For example, if your subject's hands are on the table, then also place your hands on the table, and also imitate his overall posture. This is why it is called

Chapter 2: Hypnosis Techniques

mirroring. Simply copy or mirror the other person. Now, this is only on the physical level. But, by mirroring the other person, you will soon be in sync with his mindset. This might take a bit of time but just stick to using the technique. Now, a common mistake is to just focus on the physical side of the practice. This technique is not just about copying the body position of your subject. The next thing that you want to do is to sync into the conversation. The way to do this is to simply follow the flow of the conversation that you have with your subject. Do not put up any resistance but simply go with the flow. Now, once you are physically and mentally in sync with each other, it is now your turn to take control of the conversation and give that hypnotic touch. As you can see, up to this point, it is you who is following the subject. This is to establish a connection. Now that you have this connection, you can now take control of it and lead the subject to do your will. So, how do you do this? Well, this might take some practice, but the key is to disagree with your subject. This will catch him off guard for all along everything has been in fair agreement. If you suddenly disagree, the subject will surely be caught off guard and will have almost no choice but to agree with whatever you have to say. This might not work all the time, but it can work more than 90% of the time. Now, to further increase your rate of success, you can also use other hypnotic techniques in this book. The key here is that by mirroring a person, you are able to establish a connection. Once you have that connection, you take advantage of it to hypnotize your subject.

Incrementalism

Incrementalism is about making small changes. It is not that easy to make a big change right away, so it is best to start out small. For example, if you want to lose weight, it might be too demanding to say that you should spend an hour of exercise at the gym, especially if you are not fond of doing exercises. So, instead of expecting or requiring too much, you can start by aiming for something that is easy to do, such as using the stairs instead of the escalator or elevator. Also, by making simple changes, you can start to see and feel small changes, which can encourage you to do even more. Take note that the same applies to other people. So, instead of telling someone to do everything right away, be kind enough to ask for something simple first, and be sure to show your appreciation if the person is able to do it.

Chapter 2: Hypnosis Techniques

This technique works both for hypnotizing other people, as well as for self-hypnosis. As the saying goes, "A journey of a thousand miles starts with a single step." Incrementalism is that single step. It does not have to be a difficult one; the important thing is that it should get you moving forward toward your goal.

It is good to use this technique when you want to give motivation to someone. A good example of this is if a person wants to lose weight. Although he might be aiming for something too ideal (which is good), you can encourage him to do something simple. If he loses even just a pound of weight, then express your appreciation. Motivation is important to this technique. However, before you can show appreciation and boost a person's motivation, he first needs to take positive actions. This is why you do not need to impose a difficult challenge right away. Instead, make it easily doable so that the subject would not have a hard time to do it. Once the subject is more motivated, then he will be ready to take on more difficult challenges.

Hypnosis

Positive Thinking

This is not a technique per se, but it is something that you need to observe throughout any hypnotic act. You have to think positive. This is also the way to fill yourself with positive energy. Do not hypnotize anyone to do something bad as they will most probably realize it and snap out of a hypnotic induction. This is because their mind will rebel against your words. No matter how hypnotically induced someone is, you do not tell him to steal money from someone else or to kill someone. It just will not work. Instead, stick to positive things, for such things are easily accepted by the mind.

Also, as a hypnotist, you should have confidence in what you are doing. You cannot execute any of these techniques effectively if you have doubts in your mind. Be positive. Being positive also means treating your subject nicely. Take note that in a hypnotic act, the subject has to be as relaxed as possible, and this will not be possible if the subject is feeling controlled or manipulated in any way. Instead, make him feel relaxed by having him feel positive energy. Of course, to do this, you should have a positive and kind composure. This is something that you cannot

Chapter 2: Hypnosis Techniques

fake or act out. Instead, you should really have a positive character.

To build confidence in yourself as a hypnotist, you should engage in regular practice of these techniques. Again, learning hypnotism is just like learning a new skill, and so it demands lots of practice. Another helpful tip to think positively is to have positive or good intentions. If your intentions are good, then good thoughts also follow.

It should also be noted that positive thinking is not about deluding yourself and not recognizing the negative things in life. Rather, it is about facing life's challenges in a positive spirit. These days, positive thinking has become very popular; hence, the saying, "Think positive." Although many people know about this, only a few truly understand its meaning, and much less are those who are able to practice it in their life. So, what exactly is positive thinking? Positive thinking is having a shift in perspective of the same reality. Is the cup half full or half empty? You decide.

Gentle Touch

According to a study, you can increase your chances of having a person do you a favor if you touch him during the time that you ask for a favor. For example, instead of just saying, "Get me a coffee." You could get close to your subject, touch him on the shoulder, and say, "Could you please get me a coffee?" As you can see, being polite is also important. This is simply hard to resist. Resisting would make him look rude and nobody wants to be rude. Now, do not put so much emphasis on touching the subject. Just do it casually. The focus has to be in the words that you say — your favor and the touch should be made discreetly but make sure that he feels it. Although he may not be aware of it consciously since he will be more focused on the favor that you are asking, his subconscious mind will recognize the touch as if someone is saying "please," and this will compel him to do you a favor.

Just a word of caution: There are people who do not like being touched. In this case, you should avoid using this strategy. Hence, to be safe, before you use this approach, try to notice first if the person likes being touched or not. But, how do you do this? Well, this is actually simpler than you may think. All that you need to do is to see how the subject treats other people. If he also enjoys touching others, then chances are that he

Chapter 2: Hypnosis Techniques

would not mind being touched as well. Needless to say, when you touch your subject, be sure to be decent, and avoid any sensual touches.

Sensual Approach

Okay, this might surprise you but being sensual can be an effective way to capture attention and engage your subject. However, this would only work on people who enjoy some sensuality. Yes, this involves some touch of lust. You do this by flirting with a person. Okay, there are no strict rules when it comes to flirting, but you need to be cautious about it; otherwise, the subject might end up disappointed. Also, do not flirt too much. Although this technique promotes some sensual approach, do not forget that your objective is still to hypnotize the person and make him/her do what you will. Now, do not be too sensual. Just a hint of sensuality is enough. Once you notice that the subject is interested, then it will be easy for you to give suggestions, even direct suggestions.

Be careful about using this technique. Take note that this does not work on anyone. The first thing that you need to do is to find out if the subject is a sensual person or not. Although only a few books might teach you about this, it actually works. This is easier to do if you are a woman, although this also works if you are a man. All it takes is a hint of seduction. Remember not to go all in, just a hint of sensuality that is inviting and interesting enough would be fine.

Like Attracts Like

You are probably familiar with the teaching that like attracts like. If you want to the other person to be more open to you, then you should be open to him. The thing is that you will most likely get the same treatment the way you treat others. If you are kind to a person, then there is a good chance that he will also be kind to you. This may not work all the time, but it definitely works most of the time.

If you come to think about it, this hypnotic technique is actually a universal principle. It is based on the saying of Jesus "that you should do unto others as you would have them do unto you." Of course, this teaching is not exclusive to the Christian religion but also exists in all other spirituality.

Do not be discouraged if people do not treat you nicely even after you show them kindness. Do

Chapter 2: Hypnosis Techniques

not let other people change who you are. Just be thankful for the fact that you are not like the negative people in your life. If a person is full of negativity, it only shows that he is having a hard time with his life. Otherwise, there is no reason for him to act badly.

Be Polite

This is not really a technique in the sense that there is nothing technical about this. However, it should be noted that being polite can be very effective. In fact, when it comes to asking people to do something for you, being polite can get you a long way. When you ask someone for a favor, for example, be as polite as possible. Say "please" and use respectful words. How can you refuse someone who asks nicely of you? In the same way, when you ask people politely, it makes it hard to refuse. Sometimes, you do not really need to manipulate people using complicated hypnosis techniques; you just have to be polite and ask nicely.

Chapter 3: Best Practices

Now that you know the different techniques that you can use to hypnotize anyone, it is time for you to learn the best practices that you should observe to significantly increase your chances of success. Just like the techniques, these practices might also take some practice for you to truly learn and apply them effectively in your life.

✓ Continuous Practice

The way to learn the techniques is to engage in continuous practice. No matter how many books you read on hypnosis, there is no way that you can hypnotize anyone just by reading or gaining knowledge. Again, hypnosis is also a skill that you need to practice. Be sure to spend time and effort to put your knowledge into actual practice. The best way to engage in continuous practice is to make hypnosis a part of your life. This way you would not have to remind yourself every now and then that you have to practice. Instead, always use hypnosis every time that you can. The best way to practice it is by living it. Make it a part of your daily life. Use hypnosis when you are engaged in a conversation. It does not even have to be a serious conversation. Just use it whenever an opportunity presents itself. Now, a common mistake is failing to recognize that opportunity. The thing is that every encounter or engagement that you have with another person is an opportunity for you to apply hypnosis. Of course, you do not need to be a hardcore hypnotist who only cares about hypnotizing people. What this means is that you should do your best to practice the techniques since there is no way to learn them but by actual and continuous practice.

When you practice the techniques, you should not try to learn them all at once. Doing so will only make you end up learning nothing. Keep in mind the fact that being a successful hypnotist takes time and patience. If it were very easy to do, then many people would be hypnotists, but such is far from reality. Although it is easy, it takes time and effort to learn since you have to practice the techniques regularly. It is suggested that you pick a technique that you want to learn and spend days or even weeks learning that technique. The key is to expose yourself to the

Chapter 3: Best Practices

technique that you want to learn and get used to it. Once you get so used to it, then it will soon be a part of you that you can do naturally.

Remember that when it comes to learning the techniques of hypnosis, continuous practice remains a very important element to your success. Also, it should be noted that there is no end to practice as hypnosis should become a natural part of your life.

✓ Make It Smooth and Natural

You should execute the techniques smoothly and naturally. The way to do this is for you to relax. If you are not relaxed, then there will be pressure and you would not be able to execute the techniques properly. Of course, the way to learn this is to engage in continuous practice. Once a technique has become a natural part of you, then you will be able to execute it nicely. You also should let the other person notice that you are applying any hypnotic technique on him; otherwise, he will put up his defenses. After all, in a social setting, people would not want to be hypnotized and controlled by others. You should let your subject think and feel as if he were making his own free choice although the fact is that you have already influenced him significantly.

To help you execute the technique smoothly and naturally, do not stop practicing a particular technique until it is second nature to you. A common mistake is to shift to another technique without achieving mastery of the previous technique. Although it can be tempting to learn all the techniques quickly, it is not advisable to hurry. You should take as much time as you need. After all, do not forget that there is no end to practicing the techniques, so there is no reason for you to hurry.

✓ **Believe**

To be a successful hypnotist, you need to believe in yourself and what you do. Of course, this belief does not just come by convincing yourself to believe. Rather, you need to exert efforts and engage in regular practice of the techniques. In the beginning, you might have doubts even in believing if hypnosis actually works. Do not worry; that is normal. As you apply the techniques and learn more about hypnotism, you will start to believe and appreciate learning

Chapter 3: Best Practices

hypnotism, especially once you see that the techniques actually work.

It should be noted that you do not rely on blind faith. The best way to believe is to give the techniques time and effort. Soon enough, you will see how effectively the work, and that is the time when you can actually appreciate them. This is how you believe, by building confidence based on actual results and not just because you have read something about it. The best way is to have an actual and direct experience of hypnosis, and the only way to do this is to put it into practice.

Now, keep in mind that just because a technique does not work when you try it out does not mean that you should not believe in it anymore. Again, you should give it more time and effort. Learning how to hypnotize people is just like learning a new skill — it takes time and practice. Take, for example, a person who wants to learn how to juggle balls. Even if he has the complete instructions on how to do it, and even if he memorizes the steps, chances are that he will fail his first attempts. The important thing is not to stop practicing, because it is only through regular practice that you can learn to truly believe in yourself and in what you do.

✓ Practice Self-Hypnosis

Many people think hypnosis always involves at least two people. However, as you already know by now, you can also use hypnosis on yourself, all on your own. If you are serious about learning hypnosis, then you should take into consideration the practice of self-hypnosis as you can learn a great deal about it. After all, how can you expect to apply hypnosis successfully on others if you cannot even apply it on yourself? This book has given you several techniques to induce self-hypnosis, you just have to practice them regularly.

Self-hypnosis is actually a very important part of hypnosis. In fact, there are those who learn hypnosis who end up just mastering self-hypnosis. This is because once you know how to hypnotize yourself, you will find that there is no need to hypnotize others. By making adjustments on yourself, you can get along well with others.

It can also be said that it is easier to do self-hypnosis than controlling others. Remember

Chapter 3: Best Practices

that consent is important in any hypnotic act. Since you will be hypnotizing yourself, then you would not have to worry about gaining consent from another. Still, if you master self-hypnosis, you can use it to influence the people around you. This is one of the best things about self-hypnosis. Simply by changing yourself you can create positive changes around you. What is more, you do not have to worry about dealing with other people, not to mention people have different levels "hypnotizability." If you are just starting out, then it is strongly encouraged that you practice self-hypnosis.

✓ Proper Focus

When you apply the techniques, be sure to focus properly. A common mistake is to focus on the fruits or the intended results of your actions instead of the actions themselves. You have to realize that the intended result, which is being able to hypnotize the subject, will materialize on its own as long as you execute the actions correctly. However, if you focus on the fruits of your actions, then chances are that you may not be able to execute the techniques effectively.

You should also understand that focusing on the techniques is different from focusing on focusing on the techniques. The right way to focus on the techniques is to actually apply them and not to keep telling yourself that you need to focus. Take note that to focus demands positive action on your part. So, the next time that you apply a hypnotic technique, be sure to focus on the actions and not on the fruit of your actions.

✓ **Combine the techniques**

You can also combine the techniques to give a stronger suggestion or message. If you think that the subject is not yet that influenced, then you can influence him more by applying more techniques at the same time. Needless to say, this requires substantial amount of training on your part in order to pull this off successfully. Take note that you can combine techniques, but you should stick to giving the same suggestion to your subject. Otherwise, there is chance that he might get confused and not know which message to follow. Do not feed another suggestion to the subject unless you are sure that he is already under the first suggestion. It is also good to enforce the suggestion that you have already given him from time to time. Again, all that you

Chapter 3: Best Practices

need to do is to hypnotize him and remind him of the suggestion that you have already given him.

✓ **Build Trust**

In any hypnotic act, building trust is important. If the subject does not trust you, then he will have defenses which will prevent you from penetrating his mind. Hence, you need to build trust. The more that the subject trusts you the more that you can give him suggestions. So, how do you build trust? Well, there are no hard and fast rules on this matter. This is all about getting along well and making him feel good spending time with you. As you do this, you can use hypnosis to more easily gain his trust. Another suggested and effective way to build trust is to talk about the other person's interest and make him feel good talking with you about it. Of course, another very important element of building trust is to be true to the person. There is no better way of ruining a relationship than being caught lying or taking advantage of him. To gain trust, then be sure that you deserve it. The way to do this is to be trustworthy. This means that you need to be sincere in building a good relationship with the person and not because you want to unduly control or manipulate him. Hypnotizing people is not always a bad thing as long as you have good intentions for doing so. After all, hypnotic techniques are being used all around you, even businesses and the media are very active in the use of hypnosis although they do not refer to it using the term *hypnosis*. It is also noteworthy that you should not allow trust to be broken. Once it is broken, it is almost impossible to restore it. This is why even though you use hypnosis, it is advised that you never use it to abuse people. You should also consider the consequences of your actions. Although you may be able to influence and even control someone to do your will, it does not mean that the subject could no longer take time sooner or later to realize what happened. Take note that hypnosis does not exempt or protect you from the consequences of your actions.

✓ Active Listening

Hypnosis is not just about talking to your subject and giving suggestions. Another important part of any hypnotic act but is unfortunately overlooked is actively listening to your subject. This is a very important part so be sure to apply

Chapter 3: Best Practices

it properly. Now, the problem is that many would-be hypnotists are poor listeners. Take note that it is not just applying the techniques that matter, but you should also have a good understanding of your subject.

Now, what you need as a hypnotist is not only to listen but to actively listen to your subject. What is active listening? It is when you do not just listen but also engage the subject. Simply put, you should also make the person feel that you are honestly listening to him. Now, there are some points that you need to know to do active listening. For starters, you should ask responsive questions to your subject. This will allow your subject to be more open and explain himself better. This is easy to do; you simply have to use follow-up questions. You should also maintain eye contact. When making eye contact, avoid staring at your subject's eyes for too long as that might make him feel uneasy. Now, if you are the type who feels uncomfortable looking at a person's eyes, then you might simply stare at the corner of his eye. This will look to him as if you were staring him right in the eyes. Still, it is advised that as a hypnotist, you should get used to looking at people straight in the eyes as you can use it to employ hypnotic techniques, such the eye cue technique. It is also said that "the eyes are the windows of the soul." By learning to look at a person's eyes, you can express sincerity.

Also, by listening to your subject, you will be able to determine the best technique to use, as well as when to apply it. In fact, listening is an important part of the first phase of a hypnotic act (preparation). It is by listening that you can get to know and understand your subject. Once you know your subject, then you can take appropriate actions to be able to hypnotize him effectively.

✓ Regulate the Tone of Your Voice

You should also learn to regulate the tone of your voice. It is not just the words that you say that matter but also how you say them. So, be careful with how you talk. You can practice by listening to yourself as you talk out loud. It is advised that you find a gentle, soothing voice. Remember that hypnotism has to be made in a relaxed manner. Avoid sounding monotonous. Use not only your words but also the element of sound to hypnotize your subject. You can do this by making adjustments to the tone of your voice. You might want to listen to a storyteller and pay attention to

Chapter 3: Best Practices

how he tells stories. You will see how simple changes in the tone of one's voice can draw attention and grab the emotions of the listeners.

✓ Continuous Improvement

Always aim for continuous improvement. The science and art of hypnotism is a continuously evolving. Up to this date, there is still so much about hypnotism that remains unknown; hence, there are still people who try to uncover its amazing potential. Although this book has shared with you vital information on hypnotism, it should be noted that you should not allow this book or any other book to limit you in any way. Instead, consider this as a guide that has showed you the immense power of hypnotism. As you incorporate hypnotism into your life, you will also discover its real meaning and value. Also, do not ignore the fact that there are other people out there who are also practicing hypnotism. Feel free to join online groups and forums on the subject and meet other interesting people. This is a good way not just to gain more friends but also to learn interesting views and opinions.

Even if you are able to master all the techniques in this book, know that there are still so many things to be learned and discovered about hypnosis. Hypnosis deals with the mind, and the mind is full of mysteries and amazing potential. Again, always strive for continuous improvement.

✓ Focus on What is Good for the Subject

You should focus on what is good for your subject. You have to realize that hypnosis should not be used to unduly control people to allow you to do bad things. Keep in mind that you still cannot escape the consequences of your actions. It is also much easier to hypnotize someone if you are sincere that what you are telling him is actually good for him. The true meaning and value of hypnotism is not about scamming people or taking undue advantage of them. Rather, it is about helping yourself and others to improve and create positive changes. Only use hypnosis for good.

Conclusion

Thanks for making it through to the end of this book. We hope it was informative and able to provide you with all of the tools you need to achieve your goals whatever they may be.

The next step is to apply everything that you have learned. This book has given you the keys to effectively influence, control, and hypnotize anyone. It is up to you to turn your new-found knowledge into practice. It is also worth noting that learning how to hypnotize is a powerful ability. It is up to you how you want to use it. Still, this book strongly suggests that you only use your knowledge for good, for everything that you do has its consequences. Just because you can hypnotize people does not mean that you should take away their freewill and always impose your own. As this is a powerful skill, you should also use it wisely and carefully.

By now, you should already know that hypnosis is not a strange subject. It is well within your power to learn and master. However, it is important that after gaining the right knowledge, you should also put it into actual and regular practice.

When practicing the techniques, remember to put more focus on the quality than the number of techniques that you use. It is not the quantity but how effectively you are able to employ hypnosis and make your subject bend to your will that matter.

Now that you know what hypnosis is and the important things that you should know about it, it is time for you to actually take positive actions to make things happen. So, start putting your knowledge into actual practice and enjoy the benefits of this ancient and continuously evolving science of hypnosis.

Finally, if you found this book useful in anyway, a review on Amazon is always appreciated!

www.ingramcontent.com/pod-product-compliance
Lightning Source LLC
Chambersburg PA
CBHW020902080526
44589CB00011B/407